God's People

This book is to be returned on or before
the last date stamped below.

•Nineveh

River Tigris

River Euphrates

Babylon •

Mediterranean Sea

•Damascus

Jericho
Ashdod • •Jerusalem
Gaza• Hebron

Memphis•

Thebes•

WHERE GOD'S PEOPLE LIVED

God's People

STORIES FROM THE
OLD TESTAMENT

Retold by
GERALDINE
McCAUGHREAN

Illustrated by
ANNA C. LEPLAR

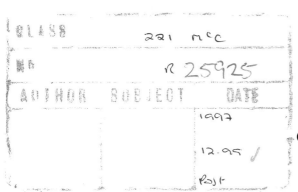

Orion Children's Books

Picture Dolphins

For Averil and Keith
G.M.

For Peter
A.C.L.

Also by Geraldine McCaughrean

Stories from Shakespeare

Myths and Legends of the World:
The Golden Hoard
The Silver Treasure
The Bronze Cauldron

First published in Great Britain in 1997
by Orion Children's Books
a division of the Orion Publishing Group Ltd
Orion House
5 Upper St Martin's Lane
London WC2H 9EA

Text copyright © Geraldine McCaughrean 1997
Illustrations copyright © Anna C. Leplar 1997
Designed by Dalia Hartman

The right of Geraldine McCaughrean and Anna C. Leplar to be
identified as the author and artist respectively of this work has been
asserted.

A catalogue record for this book is available from the British Library
Printed in Italy

CONTENTS

INTRODUCTION

THE OLD TESTAMENT is a collection of the most treasured documents of a single race of people. Amassed over a period of a thousand years, Israelite scribes writing in Hebrew (sometimes Aramaic) and living in very different parts of the Middle East recorded, in prose and poetry, their myths and legends, laws, history, the proverbs of their wisest men and the prophecies of their most revered mystics. Included are dusty court records, passionate love songs, hymns, fables and predictions about the future. Some historical parts chronicle times when the Israelites (or Hebrews) were slaves in Egypt or Babylon, others when they were a free and thriving nation.

All these varied elements come together, however, to form a surprisingly consistent picture of the God of the Israelites. While other nations are worshipping assorted carved images of their minor gods, Yaweh continues, the One True God, invisible and all-powerful, an awesome overseer and judge, demanding perfect obedience. He also comes across as the help and comforter of His Chosen People, watching over them like a father as they stumble through their difficult and dangerous lives.

The heroes of the Old Testament are not perfect; they are all too human. They make mistakes and pay for them, go astray and try to make amends. Just like us. That is why the Old Testament keeps its relevance, however far time seems to have removed us, in the modern world, from those nomads and slaves, kings, warriors and prophets of the ancient Middle East.

The scholars and poets who compiled the Old Testament included only those documents which they believed to be directly inspired by God – God steering the author's pen, as it were. For this reason, millions of people consider it holy in its very essence – a written expression of the Mind of God.

GENESIS

IN THE BEGINNING, God made the Earth and a sky overhead – sweet air instead of the breathless black of space. But the Earth was dark, unformed, clad in water. He moved over the face of the water, and gave each thing a name, without which a thing cannot be said to exist.

Just as Night draws back from Day, the waters drew back from the dry land and left continents, islands. And He saw that it was Good.

"Let the Earth grow grass and flowers and trees, crops, each plant with its own seed so that from one may grow a million and cloak the Earth with colour."

And God established Time – the turning wheel of the day, the passage of the minutes and months, the passing of the seasons, the dark sleeping world and the bright waking one. He saw that it was Good, and that Order is better than Chaos.

"Let the ocean teem with life," cried God, and in the rich salt soup of the seas there one day floated life forms – too small to see at first, one cell, then two, then worms and jellyfish, sharks and razor-shells. Soon more species swam the coral halls and mountain peaks of the seven seas than imagination can fathom. Whales as huge as islands cruised their purple territories, singing their eerie music to the stars.

In the beginning God created the heaven and the earth. And the earth was without form, and void; and darkness was upon the face of the deep.
GENESIS 1:1, 2

And God saw that it was good.
GENESIS 1:12

Birds appeared too, first with scales like fish, then feathers to cover the five-fingered bones of their wings. They colonized the cliffs, the trees, the rocks, the grassy places where larks and plovers build their nests on the ground. And all laid eggs, so that from two could come a flock and, from the flock, millions of young.

On the sixth day of Creation, God said, "Let animals live on the land." And from the smallest louse to the greatest elephant there evolved a million species to inhabit the various folds and crannies of the dry land: cattle and sheep, termites and fireflies, oxen and wildebeest, snakes and terrapins. Every creature you ever saw and many thousand more too strange for you to imagine, God created in His imagination and caused to come about, with prey for the predators, concealment for the prey.

Last of all, God created Man: a curator, a guardian of God's

So God created man in his own image, in the image of God created he him; male and female created he them.
GENESIS 1:27

Be fruitful and multiply . . . and have dominion over the fish of the sea, and over the fowl of the air.
GENESIS 1:28

Creation, with the wit to dominate all other animals and tend the Earth's plenty. As a son resembles his father, so Man resembled God – though not perhaps in looks so much as in the potential to be marvellous and good.

The name God gave to First Man was Adam, and his home was a garden planted for him in the East, a garden called Eden. It had everything in it a man could want – except a friend. So, while Adam slept, God opened his side and took a rib, and from the rib he made First Woman, or Eve. That is why women have one more rib than men, or so the story goes.

It is written that God made the Earth in six days and rested on the seventh. Remember, however, when you stand beside a fossil, or the skeleton of a dinosaur, that one day is as a thousand years in the mind of the Lord, and a thousand years as one day.

And the Lord God formed man of the dust of the ground, and breathed into his nostrils the breath of life; and man became a living soul. And the Lord God planted a garden eastward in Eden; and there he put the man whom he had formed.
GENESIS 2:7, 8

PARADISE LOST

"ALL THIS IS YOUR GARDEN," God told Adam. "You may eat any of its fruits and berries – from every tree and bush . . . except for that one there."

The tree was a fountain of blossom, a canopy of leaves, a tent of shade amid the sunlight, with fruit like plush-bloomed apples. "Don't eat the fruit from this tree, or the taste for you will be bitter indeed." Adam and Eve could barely imagine anything unpleasant – they had never felt pain or sickness, bad luck, disappointment . . . or temptation. For all that they were adult, they played in the Garden like innocent children.

A serpent lived very close by – a lizard-like creature with a proud, arching head. One day, as Eve passed by the Forbidden Tree, the snake coiled itself around the dappled trunk and beckoned her with a wave of its emerald head. "Eat-t," it said.

"God said we mustn't!"

"That's-s because He knew the fruit would make you wise – wise like the angels, wise as He is wise: Godlike. Eat-t-t. The fruit is good."

Eve did eat, and ran and told Adam to eat as well. And see? They did not fall down dead on the spot, or clutch at their stomachs in agony! "What did I s-s-say?" hissed the serpent, flickering its forked tongue. But it was pleased not for Adam and Eve's sake, but at its own cunning.

They did not feel like angels, either. Their bodies all of a sudden looked bare and rude. "Cover yourself up!" Adam shouted at his wife. "You can't go about like . . . like *that*!"

"Me?" retorted Eve. "Look at you! Naked. Indecent!"

Quickly they made themselves aprons out of fig leaves. They were no longer innocents playing in the sun. They had done what God had expressly forbidden them to do, and when they

heard Him coming – heard His footsteps on the grass at evening dewfall – they were ashamed of more than their nakedness.

Between the song of the blackbird and the singing of the nightingale, God came walking through Eden. He stopped beside the bush where Adam and Eve were crouched. "Why are you hiding from me?"

"We were ashamed to be seen in only our bare bodies," said Adam.

"Who told you you were naked?"

"No one. We . . ."

"You have done what I expressly forbad you to do. You have eaten fruit from the tree that I told you to leave untouched."

They would have given anything, then, not to have disobeyed. Because of the look in God's eyes. Nothing would ever be the same. His anger stood between them like an iron grille, a bottomless gulf, like a million years.

First God banished the snake from Eden, for tempting Eve to eat. He cursed it with curses that withered its legs and dropped its proud head to the ground. "Crawl on your belly through all eternity, and may the food in your mouth all turn to ash!"

Resentful and nursing plans for vengeance, the snake slithered out of Eden on its scaly belly.

"As for you," said God, turning to Adam and Eve, "you have lost the right to live in Eden. Leave here. The world outside is all that you deserve. Work the stony fields to raise your food, Adam. Fight with thorns and thistle for a patch of earth to grow your corn. From now on, giving birth to children will be a labour to you, Eve, dangerous and hard. Now both of you go! Live as long as you are able, and when you can no longer live, *die*! I made you from dust, and that shall be your life's reward – to turn to dust again in the grave."

Out through the eastern gate of Eden God drove First Man and First Woman, to where thorns toiled in coils out of parched,

In the sweat of thy face shalt thou eat bread, till thou return unto the ground; for out of it wast thou taken: for dust thou art, and unto dust shalt thou return.
GENESIS 3:19

stony ground. And He stationed an angel at the gate, with a burning sword, to stop them ever going back. The Forbidden Tree stood lonely in the centre of a garden visited only by bees and birds. The fruit cankered on the branches of the other trees, too, un-picked, uneaten, unenjoyed. The whole Garden was a waste of God's labour. For what is Beauty without anyone to enjoy it?

CAIN AND ABEL

ADAM AND EVE'S children were born outside the Garden. They must have heard their parents talk of it, and knew they could never go there. The two boys were called Cain and Abel. Cain chose to sow corn and harvest it, Abel to be a shepherd.

Adam and Eve had learned their lesson, and taught their sons to respect God. So at the end of lambing, Abel offered up his best lamb on an altar: a sacrifice, a thanksgiving. He set a fire, and the sweet smell of roasting meat rose straight up to Heaven. At the start of harvest, Cain too offered a stook of corn. But the stalks would not catch, the ears would not kindle. The flames turned away like a man shunning his friend.

Cain had a ready temper. He made a face and smashed at the fire with a stick. "What's the matter with my offering, eh? Not good enough for You?"

God's answer crackled in the cinders. "There is nothing wrong with your crop, Cain, but perhaps in you – or near you – lurks something unacceptable in the eyes of Heaven. Go carefully, child, for I see wickedness waiting in ambush to pounce and make you its own."

Then Cain's temper kindled white-hot, even though his corn had not. Concealing it as best he could, he asked his brother, in the friendliest way, to go walking in the fields. When they were out of sight of any living soul, he cut down Abel with a scythe. Abel fell like reaped corn, and Cain hid the dead body. But God sees everything.

The blowing corn seethed. The ripe ears hissed. "Cain! Where is your brother Abel?"

Cain shrugged. "How should I know? Is he a sheep and I his shepherd that I should look after him all day?"

And the Lord said unto Cain, Where is Abel thy brother? And he said, I know not: Am I my brother's keeper?
GENESIS 4:9

The wind worked the corn into a fury. "What have you done, Cain? Your brother's blood shouts out from the very ground! The soil curses Cain, because it has drunk his blood! It won't yield crops to you now – not this field, nor any other! Run, murderer, run! Lose yourself among the wild places of the world!"

"No!" cried Cain, clutching up clods of soil in stark terror. "Where will I go? I can't bear it! Wherever I run people will say, 'There's Cain the murderer, the man God turned His back on.' They'll kill me!"

"No, that I won't allow." So God slapped His mark on Cain's forehead, like a daub of blood. No amount of washing would remove it. Seeing the Mark of Cain, people knew him for what he was, but that God meant him to live on . . . and on . . . and on . . . wandering the world without the friendship of his own God.

NOAH AND THE FLOOD

As time passed, the family of Adam grew larger and larger. His children had children, their grand-children had grandchildren. The numbers of people on Earth grew with every generation. But although there were more people, they were no better than Cain or wiser than Eve. In fact they became so wicked that God was sorry He had ever created the human race. We all wish our mistakes undone. God chose to undo His: humankind.

Only one man deserved better. Noah was a good man. God and he were like friends. So God said to his friend, "Noah! The world has become a sordid, wicked place and I'm sorry I ever made it. I will wash it clean with a flood. So build a wooden ship – an ark – and daub the planks with pitch outside and in, to keep out water. Build it three storeys high, and take aboard your wife and three sons – oh, and their wives, too. Then find every kind of animal – a male and a female of every bird and beast – and load them on, too. Why should they die for people's sins? Don't forget provisions, mind! Plenty of food for yourselves and the animals!"

Noah did exactly as he was told, whether or not his neighbours jeered and pointed and called him a madman, pelting him with pebbles and abuse. He set about building – right there, in the middle of dry land. He and his family went aboard, but it was seven days more before the rain came.

Then in out of the wet came all the birds and beasts on Earth – two by two, as lightning tore the heavens open like a ripsaw and let fall the rain in torrents.

The rising water shifted, then lifted the ark, bumping it across the ground before setting it fully afloat. Standing at the rail, Noah saw the fields silvered over, his mud house crumbling, whole

And of every living thing . . . two of every sort shalt thou bring unto the ark, to keep them alive with thee; they shall be male and female.

Genesis 6:19

*Again he sent forth
the dove out of
the ark;
And the dove came
in to him in the
evening; and, lo, in
her mouth was an
olive leaf pluckt off:
so Noah knew that
the waters were
abated from off the
earth.*

GENESIS 8:10, 11

*I do set my bow in
the cloud, and it
shall be for a token
of a covenant
between me and
the earth.*

GENESIS 9:13

cities filled to the brim with water, and everyone – every wicked living soul – run, wade, swim, scream, then sink in the mud-brown Flood. Noah, his family, his zoo – and God – watched it happen.

When, after forty days and forty nights, the rain finally stopped, water masked the face of the Earth. Nothing broke the surface – not a rock, not a tree. Then a wind sprang up; the water steamed. The ark ran aground on the peak of Mount Ararat.

Noah freed a raven to fly away in search of something to eat, somewhere to perch. But the raven only flew up and down, up and down, finding nowhere, nothing. Noah freed a dove, but she came back exhausted. A week later, Noah sent the dove out again. And again she came back to the ark. But to Noah's delight, there was the leaf from an olive tree in her beak. Now Noah knew that the water really was dropping. After another week, Noah's dove did not come back at all: she had found somewhere better than the ark to roost. So Noah opened up the ark and everyone climbed out: Noah, his family and all the animals.

"Have children – lots of children!" God told the little family. "People the world all over again! But I promise you – no more Floods, never again such destruction." And He wrote His oath in the sky, in the shining arc of a rainbow, His everlasting promise of pity.

THE TOWER OF BABEL

IN THE EARLY DAYS of the world, all the people on Earth were of one wandering tribe – tent-dwellers in search of somewhere to build in brick and stone. The place they chose was a great plain in a land called Shinar.

But not content to build a house, or a street of houses, or a city of streets, they said, "Let's build a tower – the highest the world has ever seen. Let's build it so high that its roof bangs against Heaven and people can see it from half a world away! We shall be famous for ever!"

They could do it, too, because they all spoke the same language and could cooperate, plan, send messages from bottom to top of the tower and, above all, *think in the same words*. Their great fault was pride: the wish to be on a level with God, without first measuring up to Him in goodness.

They built, and as they built God watched with mounting anger. Between each baked brick was a mortar of slime, and a slimier layer of arrogance. "Soon we'll be equal with God!" they crowed, from on top their monumental chimneypot. "We'll be up among the angels!"

So God pulled a brick from the base of the tower, and breathed on it: *huh.*

Down it came, with the slowness of a falling tree, and shattered along the ground in a mile-long cloud of dust. All the builders who clung to its sides were hurled to the four quarters of the Shinar Plain and far beyond. And when they got to their feet and began the long walk back, they found their mouths full of dust. Calling out to their comrades, they heard their words come out as gibberish: words and accents and alphabets had all been jarred by the fall into a confusion of sound, a babble.

And they said, Go to, let us build us a city and a tower, whose top may reach unto heaven; and let us make us a name . . .
GENESIS 11:4

And I will make of thee a great nation, and I will bless thee, and make thy name great; and thou shalt be a blessing:
And I will bless them that bless thee, and curse him that curseth thee: and in thee shall all families of the earth be blessed.
GENESIS 12:2, 3

And that is how the tower gained its name, how Language broke into a thousand different languages, and how men were parted from each other for ever by the difference.

SARAH'S SON

THE DAY'S heat melted the desert landscape. The air above the hot ground wavered and made solid things look vaporous and unreal. The three figures walking towards Abraham's tent seemed to hover, semi-transparent.

Hospitality is the first law of the desert, and he hurried out to greet them, bow respectfully and offer them rest and refreshment. While they sat down under the shade of a tree, he hurried back to his wife. "We have visitors, Sarah! Bake three of your special cakes and I'll kill a calf and roast it."

It would not have been modest for Sarah to show herself, so she did her cooking out of sight, inside the tent. That did not stop her listening to the conversation: she was as interested as Abraham to hear travellers' news, stories and gossip.

"Where's Sarah your wife?" asked one of the strangers.

"How did you know . . . ? She's in the tent," said Abraham, taken aback.

"Well, we have some news for her – for you both. She is going to have a baby – a son."

At that, Sarah put her floury hands over her mouth and laughed a silent bitter laugh. "Oh, am I indeed?" she thought cynically. "At my age?"

Outside, the stranger suddenly said, "Why did Sarah laugh?"

"I didn't hear anything," said Abraham, though he felt like laughing himself at the absurd notion of Sarah having a baby. He knew perfectly well that she was way past the age for having children. He sent for her, nevertheless, to see if she had laughed.

"Laugh? I didn't laugh!" blustered Sarah.

"Yes, you did," insisted the stranger, "and you thought to yourself, 'At my age? Old enough to be a grandmother, and childless all my married life. That will be the day!' "

And the Lord said unto Abraham, Wherefore did Sarah laugh . . . ? Is any thing too hard for the Lord?
GENESIS 18:13, 14

Sarah blushed. "Wee-e-ll. Who ever heard such nonsense! Look at me. I'm an old woman!"

"Sarah," said the stranger. "Is anything too hard for God? As for you, Abraham, you shall become more than the father of a son. God has it in mind to make you the father of a nation, the Pole Star in a sky of numberless stars." Then the three ate their meal in silence, watched in awe by two old people crouched in the doorway of a humble desert tent.

The baby was real enough, even so. He was born nine months later: Isaac, the dearest gift God could ever have given to Abraham and Sarah. As she cradled him in her arms, Sarah laughed – a huge, hearty, long, loud laugh – out of sheerest joy.

SODOM AND GOMORRAH

"WHERE ARE YOU HEADED?" Abraham asked the strangers who had brought him such good news.

"To the twin cities on the plain. To Sodom and Gomorrah."

"I shall start you on your way. And when you are in Sodom, you must stay with my nephew Lot. It's a wicked place, but you'll be safe with him."

"Wicked, yes. The stench of it rankles in God's nostrils. But not for long. Soon Sodom and Gomorrah will be nothing but rubble." On the brink of a ridge they left Abraham, and strode on effortlessly down the shaly slopes, towards the coastal plain of the salty Dead Sea. Angels. Abraham wondered why he had not realized it before.

Distance lent beauty to Sodom and Gomorrah, clustered hives of honey-coloured buildings, their roofs and awnings catching the sun. Abraham turned his face to the sky. "No, Lord! You can't! You wouldn't! Destroy Sodom and Gomorrah? After the Flood you said . . . No! Wipe out men, women and children, good and bad alike? I know most of them are evil, but maybe fifty of them are good, God-fearing . . ."

"If there are fifty good people living in Sodom, I will not destroy the city," said God's voice.

Abraham was relieved. Then he began to have misgivings. "What if there weren't quite fifty?"

"If there are forty-five good people, I won't destroy Sodom."

Abraham was satisfied. Almost. "What about thirty?"

"For the sake of thirty I would hold off."

"Twenty?"

"For the sake of twenty I would spare the cities."

Abraham chewed his beard nervously. "I know I'm nothing,

Because the cry of Sodom and Gomorrah is great, and because their sin is very grievous; I will go down . .
GENESIS 18:20-21

nobody, but listen . . . What if there are ten?"

"For the sake of ten good people, I would spare Sodom."

Abraham breathed out slowly and smiled. There must be ten: there was all of Lot's household, for a start.

• • •

Lot met by chance the strangers who had just visited Abraham. He did not recognize them as angels, either, at first, but immediately offered them food and a bed for the night. No sooner did the word spread of his visitors than all the local louts came slouching and shouting round Lot's house. Their mouths were full of swearwords. Their heads were full of swearwords. Their lives were like swearwords, coarse and brutish.

When Lot went out to reason with them, they turned on him instead. "Well, if we can't have them, we'll make do with you!" they jeered, jolting him up against his own front door. The door opened. The visitors snatched Lot inside to safety. And perhaps

they threw something – a handful of salt? – into the eyes of the hooligans outside. For the ones at the front staggered backwards, clutching their eyes, saying they could not see, fumbling for the door without finding it.

"Pack your things and go," the angels told Lot. "Sodom is damned and Gomorrah is doomed."

Lot told his wife and two daughters. He told the boys who had married his daughters, too. But they did not believe him. Sodom fall? To whose army? For what?

At dawn the angel-visitors urged Lot out of his house. "Hurry. There's no time left. Run and keep running, and whatever happens – *don't look back!*"

Lot snatched hold of his wife's wrist, she of her elder daughter's hand, the daughter grabbed her sister by the plait, and away they went led by the strangers through the deserted streets to the city gate.

"My house! My things!" protested Lot's wife. But they ran, all

For we will destroy this place . . . and the Lord hath sent us to destroy it.
GENESIS 19:13

Escape for thy life; look not behind thee . . . lest thou be consumed.
GENESIS 19:17

the same, out of the gates on to the plain, scattering sheep, startling the dawn birds into flight. The earth quaked under their running feet. *"Don't look back!"* yelled Lot.

Then it began to rain: gouts of fire, spurts of pitch, gobbets of sulphurous incandescent rock. It was as if the Earth had began to purge itself, to spit up foulness and fire from its stomach and vomit it down on Sodom. Straw strewings kindled, awnings flapped in flames, turrets fell on to upturned swearing faces. Sulphur poured out of the sky in yellow, syrupy cataracts. Smoke belched black and stinking along the narrow alleyways, choking and stifling, blinding and smothering, silencing the swearing. God excised the cities of Sodom and Gomorrah, and the firestorm cauterized the open wounds. Some few miles away, the Dead Sea heaved and overflowed.

"My home! My friends!" wailed Lot's wife, and she shook off his hot hands, broke free of her daughters – and glanced back.

What she saw turned her face pale. What she witnessed turned her hair grey. But what she had *done*, in disobeying, turned her hands and arms and legs and body white, too. A whirl of sharp salt whipped off the Dead Sea to pelt and envelop her. It caked her eyes, filled her mouth, struck her flesh so hard that it changed substance. Between her running husband and her lagging daughters, she turned to salt – first in female shape, then to a pillar, a slab of rock salt licked by the tongues of fire still falling out of the sky. Lot never even saw it happen. His face was towards the nearby town of Zoar and the shelter it would offer his dear family . . .

• • •

Abraham looked down on the coastal plain next day and watched the smoke curl and coil over the ruins. From a distance they looked like twin brick kilns, or two hives filled with smoke to empty them of bees. "Not ten," he said to himself. "Not even ten."

THE SACRIFICE OF ISAAC

SOME EIGHT YEARS LATER, at the tail end of a restless night, Abraham heard the voice of God speaking in his dreams. "Abraham, take your boy, your only son Isaac, to the mountains of Moriah, and build a priestly altar there to me. Sacrifice your son on that altar. Spill his blood and burn his dead body, that I may smell the sweet smoke of holy sacrifice."

Abraham woke himself up by crying out, but he said nothing to his wife, nothing to Isaac. He simply loaded an ass with firewood, took a cleaver, a rope and tinder, and called his son to his side. It took three days to reach Moriah, and every mile must have been an agony to Abraham, his secret banging against his heart like the cleaver banging against his thigh. At the bottom of the mountain they had to leave the ass while Isaac carried the firewood on his back.

"I've got the wood, and you've got the knife and the rope and fire, Father," said the little boy, "but where's the animal for us to kill?"

"God will provide that, my son," said Abraham, though the words stuck in his throat like dry pebbles.

On a high, level place, Abraham built an altar out of sharp rocks, piling them up with care. "But Father, what *are* we going to offer up to God on this altar of ours?" asked Isaac.

"You!"

He caught hold of Isaac and tied him tight with the rope — it must have been hard to tie knots with his eyes full of tears. He laid his Isaac, his only son, the miracle of his old age, on the stony altar. He reached out for the knife, turning his son's head away so as not to see the look in his eyes. The blade of the cleaver glinted in the low sun as Abraham lifted it . . .

And he said, Take now thy son, thine only son Isaac, whom thou lovest . . . and offer him there for a burnt offering upon one of the mountains which I will tell thee of.
GENESIS 22:2

And Abraham stretched forth his hand, and took the knife to slay his son.
GENESIS 22:10

THE SACRIFICE OF
ISAAC

*And in thy seed
shall all the nations
of the earth be
blessed . . .*
GENESIS 22:18

"Abraham! Abraham!" The words rolled down the mountainside like loose rocks. "Don't kill your son. Let him go. God knows now that you are ready to obey Him, at any price — even at the cost of your dearest joy. You were ready to give up your son, your own and only son."

The voice was gradually drowned out by a loud bleating nearby. Abraham turned round and saw a ram caught by its horns in a thornbush. He untied Isaac and together they laid the ram on the stony altar: it must have been a struggle, with trembling arms and legs like water. Then Isaac helped his aged father down the thorny mountainside. The ram as it burned sent up a sweet-smelling smoke into the sky behind them.

Year by year, God rewarded his obedient servant Abraham with prosperity, success and growing influence. It is not recorded what Isaac thought about the test.

Was it too much to ask? Too cruel a test? Far too much, far too cruel. Unless God Himself were willing to embark on that same wilderness journey and see His son, His own and only son, put to death on a lonely hillside, like some sacrificial lamb.

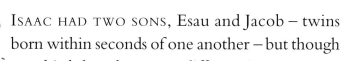

JACOB AND ESAU

ISAAC HAD TWO SONS, Esau and Jacob – twins born within seconds of one another – but though they shared the same birthday, they were different in every way. Esau had shaggy ginger hair; even his arms and legs were as woolly as a goat. He liked to hunt deer in the mountains, and Isaac loved him for his manly daring. Jacob, on the other hand, never strayed far from the tents. He tended the animals and kept his mother, Rebekah, company so that she doted on him with a fierce, smothering love. Unlike Esau he was a pale, smooth boy – smooth, you might say, in more than skin.

God had let Rebekah know, ahead of time, that her twin sons would found two great tribes, but that one son would be master over the other. She meant Jacob to be that master, and went about making sure he was. But it was not going to be easy. Esau had been born first – only by seconds, but first, even so. In law, he was the firstborn son, and Isaac's heir.

One day, Esau came in from hunting, famished and weary. Jacob had made a lentil stew, and the delicious smell billowed through the tents. "Give me a bowl of that, eh?" said Esau flopping down. "I'm just about fit to drop."

"What's it worth?" said Jacob.

"Come on, give it me. I'd give anything just now for a good meal."

"I'll settle for your birthright," said Jacob.

Esau was too tired to move, and perhaps he thought it was a joke. "Well, my birthright won't do me much good if I die of hunger, will it? Have it."

"Swear!" said Jacob, with a ferocity which startled his brother.

"All right! You can be the firstborn! Now give me the stew, will you?"

And the boys grew: and Esau was a cunning hunter, a man of the field; and Jacob was a plain man, dwelling in tents.
GENESIS 25:27

Jacob set down the bowl and brought his brother a drink besides. But from that day forwards he considered himself the elder son and heir. Esau had sold his birthright for a plate of stew.

But old Isaac still loved Esau best and what is a birthright in comparison with a father's blessing?

In those days, a blessing was a gift every bit as tangible as a plate of food. A father's love might warm the air around his children like sunlight. But his dying *blessing* was something entirely different. It was a transfer of goods and of good fortune.

One day, when Isaac was old and blind and sensed his death was not far off, he called Esau to him. "Go and hunt deer, son, and prepare me roast venison. I'm never happier than when I'm eating venison hunted by my own dear boy. When you bring that meal, I'll give you my dying blessing."

Rebekah, always eavesdropping, overhead this. "Jacob! Go and kill two baby kids, and I'll make a meal so good your father will think it's venison. And put on these clothes of Esau's – don't argue, just do it."

When she had cooked the goat's meat, she scraped the skins clean and tied furry strips to the backs of Jacob's smooth hands, and the nape of his smooth neck. "Now, go and receive his blessing: he'll only give it once."

"What if he isn't fooled?" protested Jacob (though he did not shake off the goatskin mittens). "He may curse me instead of blessing me!"

"Then let the curse fall on me," said Rebekah briskly, as if she were talking about a shower of rain, and thrust the stewpot into his hands.

So, for a second time, Jacob served up a meal to trick the eater. "I've brought you venison, Father, so that you'll grant me a father's blessing."

"You were quick!" exclaimed Isaac, reaching out blindly towards his son. He was ill at ease. "You feel and smell like Esau, but you sound more like Jacob. Is it really you, Esau my boy?"

"It is," lied Jacob. "Bread, Father? Let me pour you some wine."

Then Isaac laid his old hands on Jacob's goatskin mittens and on the furry nape of his neck. "May God give as much prosperity as He has given me, with many children and all good fortune. Everything I have is yours."

A tent flap rattled. Esau was home, dragging a deer behind

him by its antlers. Jacob crept away, clutching the blessing to him like stolen property.

Esau prepared the real venison stew and took it in. "I've brought you venison, Father, so that you'll grant me a father's blessing!"

Isaac trembled and pulled himself to his feet: "Someone has tricked me! I've given away the blessing I meant for you!"

Esau gave a cry so loud and bitter that it soured the water in the well. *You could bless me, too, surely!*

"No. A father has only one blessing to give, and I have given all my goods and good wishes to your brother."

"First my birthright, now my blessing . . . Is there nothing left for me?"

"Nothing but to serve your brother; I've bound you to that. But one day, I prophesy, you shall break free of his service."

No comfort to a man just cheated of everything by his own brother. Esau hated Jacob with venomous loathing, and vowed to kill him. Rebekah realized as much, and told Jacob to go – and go far – out of the reach of Esau's revenge. She even made up an excuse for him to leave.

Next day, Isaac summoned Jacob to his bedside. "Your mother has a poor opinion of the girls in these parts. She wants you to marry someone from her own country. So go to your Uncle Laban's place and let him find you a suitable bride." Extraordinarily, he spoke no word of bitterness, but fresh blessings to tide Jacob on his way. And so it seemed that the trickster would prosper, and have his way in everything. But Jacob was about to meet a man after his own nature. He would need all his cunning if his good fortune was to continue.

JACOB'S LADDER

ON HIS WAY to Laban's settlement, Jacob lay down and slept, his head pillowed on stones. He dreamed that a ladder stood propped against the clouds. Angels were climbing the ladder, and at the top stood God, speaking Jacob's destiny: "This land, where you've laid your head, I will give to you and to your descendants. This stony bed and everything to North, South, East and West, as far as the horizon, shall belong to you and yours. And you shall have children and grandchildren enough to settle it, too, because I have decided to bless you with a father's blessing." (Extraordinarily, he spoke no word of reproach concerning Esau.)

When Jacob woke, he was convinced he had slept at the very gate of Heaven.

• • •

Before he even met his uncle, Jacob knew which of Laban's family he wanted to marry. A muddle of sheep were pushing and jostling around a covered well where Jacob paused to ask directions. The lid of the well was too heavy to lift for the women who daily brought their flocks to drink there; they had to wait until someone strong came by. Rachel, Jacob's cousin, was one such shepherdess.

As soon as Jacob caught sight of her, he fell in love: he even kissed her! His heart thumping with excitement, he pushed the lid aside, with a great show of manly strength, and watered all Rachel's sheep. While he heaved the stone back into place, she ran ahead to say who was coming. And her father Laban gave him such a welcome, you would have thought Jacob was his long-lost son.

"You can't possibly work for me for nothing! I must pay you a wage!" he volunteered. "What shall it be?"

And he dreamed, and behold a ladder set up on the earth, and the top of it reached to heaven: and behold the angels of God ascending and descending on it.
GENESIS 28:12

"I'll work seven years as a shepherd, sir, if you'll let me marry Rachel."

Laban glanced in the direction of his womenfolk, and his eyes flickered. "Agreed! Seven years and she's yours!"

Seven years? It seemed like seven days, Jacob was so much in love. Seven years? It seemed like seven thousand years before he could call Rachel his own. Her sister Leah was beautiful, with eyes like a fawn, but Rachel by comparison was the sun beside a candle, a star beside a stone.

On his wedding day, Jacob was the happiest man alive. He danced and sang all day with the men (as was the custom), then, as night fell, crept into the bridal tent to claim his bride. "Are you there, my love, my dearest?"

"I'm here," replied a voice in the darkness.

In the morning, when Jacob woke, a woman's dark hair was spilling across his pillow. But it was not Rachel's dark hair. Leah lay sleeping beside him. For once the trickster had been tricked.

Jacob raged over to his uncle's tent and shook it till the poles broke. Laban stuck out his head, as wide-eyed as his daughter and quite unabashed. "It's just not the custom round here, you see, to let the younger daughter marry first. Now if it's Rachel you want . . ."

Seven years more, seven years of shepherding Jacob had to promise to Laban, in return for Rachel. But he swore to work those seven years, and so won the bride of his choice. In those days, a man could take as many wives as he could support. But Rachel and Leah were quite enough for any man. They competed ferociously for Jacob's love. Leah prided herself that she was the better wife, because, for a long time, only she bore Jacob sons. But Jacob's true love only ever belonged to Rachel.

So important were children to a man in those days, that both women had their serving maids bear children for Jacob as well. Thus the tribe of Jacob grew enormous in a very few years. Sons

were born to Jacob like so many almonds falling from the tree: a whole tribe of handsome sons. But at that time only Joseph was born to Rachel herself, so that when Jacob looked at his sons, he saw in only one Rachel's sweet face smiling back at him.

And he loved Joseph best.

· · ·

Though life treated him well, after fourteen years Jacob's thoughts turned towards home. He wanted more from life than to be a hired man, tending sheep, working for his uncle. There again, he saw no reason to leave empty-handed. He had built up Laban's wealth of cattle, goats and sheep into a flock so large it smothered the hillside like an avalanche. As he said to Laban, "I'm surely entitled to some animals of my own, now that I'm going?"

Laban smiled his broad, generous smile: "But of course!"

Cunning Jacob smiled back. "Well then, dear Uncle, give me all the calves and kids born this season with spots or stripes or blotches, and all the brown lambs."

Laban's calculating brain rattled like an abacus. Piebald animals were not so common, after all. And Laban supposed he could spare a few of the brown lambs.

When the deal was struck, Jacob hurried away and cut green twigs, whittled off some of the bark, and "planted" them all round the sheepfold. The ewes saw the speckled twigs (or else God sided once more with Jacob) and all the best calves and kids born that season were spotted, or striped or blotched. Every lamb was brown. To give Laban his due, he stuck by their bargain.

Surrounded by his wives, his children and his dappled flock, Jacob moved away across the desert like the shadow of a large, slow-moving cloud. An uncertain welcome awaited him in the land of his birth. Would those rough and hairy hands of Esau be outstretched in welcome or brandishing a sword?

JACOB WRESTLES WITH GOD

A MAN WHO HAS cheated his brother does not look forward to a family reunion. Though Jacob wanted to go home to the land of his birth, he was exceedingly nervous of meeting Esau, whom he had cheated out of both birth-right and father's blessing. Mustering his enormous family of wives, maidservants and children, he had them travel in front of him, and primed them to say to anyone they met, "We are of Jacob's family. He's coming with a present for his dear brother Esau."

One evening, at a river ford, he sent his family and flocks over ahead of him and stayed behind alone. Alone? Not quite, for all of a sudden a stranger appeared and demanded to wrestle with him. Hand to hand, forehead to forehead, straining and grunting, the two men fought. The blood roared in Jacob's ears, the sweat poured down his body. He shrugged off his cloak and robe and fought, on, flesh against flesh. His adversary had massive strength, but Jacob had his womenfolk and children to think of and, like a stag protecting his does and fawns, he was ready to fight on and on. Locked in combat, they danced the violent dance of wrestlers, striving to hook away a leg, to catch the other off-balance. Grappling without word or cry, they rolled in and out of the icy river.

*Thy name shall be
called no more
Jacob, but Israel:
for as a prince hast
thou . . . prevailed.*

GENESIS 32:28

All night they wrestled, and when the stranger saw that he would never force his opponent to submit, he simply reached down and touched Jacob's thigh. No more. Not a blow, simply a touch.

Jacob fell to the ground with a cry, his thigh muscle shrunk, the strength gone from his leg. But he took the other man down with him, his arms clasping the stranger's body, his hands binding him like manacles.

"Let me go. It is nearly dawn," said the stranger suddenly. He was not even breathless.

"No, I shan't let you go. Not until you bless me."

"How can I bless you, unless you tell me your name?"

"My name is Jacob."

"Not any longer," said the stranger. "For that means 'supplanter', 'usurper'. Your name shall be Israel – 'he struggled with God' – because you have won all your fights."

"And what's *your* name?" asked Jacob . . . or rather Israel.

"Why ask?"

Suddenly the stranger was gone, and Jacob lay exhausted on the riverbank. "I was afraid to see my brother's face, and instead I've seen God's!" Then he pulled himself painfully to his feet and waded across the river, limping on his sprained thigh.

Soon after, he saw a huge force of men coming towards him. It was Esau and Esau's cohort of fighting men. The brothers approached one another, Jacob warily, but Esau bounding forward in the great strides of a soldier.

"I've brought you a present to say how very sorry . . ." began Jacob.

"Keep it. Keep your present," said Esau flinging his arms round his brother's neck. "God's been good to me since you left. I've prospered – just as you've obviously done to judge by all these wives and children. And now we're together again! The twin sons of Isaac are reunited at last!"

JOSEPH AND HIS COAT OF MANY COLOURS

LUCKY JOSEPH, to be his father's favourite son. The result was that his older brothers hated him. Lucky Joseph, to be blessed with special powers, to be a dreamer and a reader of dreams. The result was that he infuriated, scared and affronted people. Lucky Joseph, to be destined for dizzy heights of fame. To reach them he must first endure exile, slavery and prison.

When Jacob gave his favourite son a beautiful new coat, his ten older brothers seethed with envy. This was not a skimpy, everyday shepherd's jacket, but a robe with long sleeves and full, billowing folds falling to the very thongs of his sandals. Its woollen weft was brightly dyed, and no one else had a coat like it.

"I dreamt a dream last night," Joseph told his brothers, pulling on the coat delightedly. "I dreamed we were tying up sheaves of corn at harvest-time, and suddenly all your sheaves gathered round mine and bowed down to it." (It was not a dream likely to please Joseph's brothers.) "Do you want to hear another? I dreamt the sun and moon and eleven stars all bowed down to me!"

Even Jacob resented *that* dream. The eleven stars were plainly Joseph's eleven brothers, including baby Benjamin. That meant the sun and moon must be his mother and father. "So you think your mother and I will bow down to you one day, do you?" said Jacob indignantly.

"I just dreamed it," said Joseph.

One day, Jacob sent Joseph to see all was well with his brothers, out among the hills where they grazed the family sheep. They saw him coming at a great distance; there was no mistaking that bright, billowing coat.

And he dreamed yet another dream, and told it to his brethren, and said, Behold, I have dreamed a dream more; and, behold, the sun and the moon and the eleven stars made obeisance to me.
GENESIS 37:9

*And they said one
to another, Behold,
this dreamer
cometh.*
GENESIS 37:19

*And he knew it,
and said, It is my
son's coat; an evil
beast hath devoured
him; Joseph is
without doubt rent
in pieces.*
GENESIS 37:33

"Here comes the dreamer," said Simeon. "It wouldn't worry
me if that boy met with a nasty accident one of these days. What
say we arrange one?"

"No! Spill a brother's blood?" said Reuben. "That would be
. . . unlucky. We should throw him into some pit and leave him
there." (Reuben was a good man, and seeing his brothers were
bent on mischief, hoped to be able to come back later and rescue
Joseph, despite them.)

Grabbing hold of Joseph, they tore off his beautiful coat and
pitched him into a deep, empty, dry cleft in the rocky ground.
Then they moved well away to eat their midday meal, so as not
to hear his shouts: "Simeon? Dan? Asher? What have I done?
Help me! Don't leave me here to die of thirst!"

Just then, a caravan of camels came into sight, moving through
the heat haze like a ship through water. "Look!" said Judah. "Here's
our chance to make some money. Let's sell the dreamer to those
merchants. Then we'll be rid of him without having his blood on
our consciences!" Reuben was out of sight, busy with one of his
sheep. The other brothers were quick to agree.

So Joseph was sold for twenty pieces of silver, and led away on
a rope's end like any of the other animals in the caravan train.
The brothers killed a goat and daubed its blood on the beautiful
long-sleeved coat, then set off for home. When Reuben, unaware
of what had happened, went back to the pit to haul Joseph out,
he found to his horror that the pit was empty.

"Look what we found, Father! It looks like Joseph's coat. We
hope nothing has happened to him," said the brothers. Jacob
grabbed the bright woollen cloth and clutched it to his cheek.
Tears spilled from his lashes.

"Are you blind? Don't you see the blood? My boy's been
eaten by some wild animal! My poor dear Joseph is dead!" And
he rocked and sobbed and tore his clothes in grief. Nothing his
sons said could comfort him.

Meanwhile, Joseph was travelling down to Egypt – the Egypt of the Pharaoh-kings – alone and afraid, for sale along with gum and myrrh and sweet spices.

Potiphar, a captain in Pharaoh's guard, bought him. He took an immediate liking to Joseph, who could turn his hand to anything, and trusted him more and more with the running of the house. Joseph never let him down. Unfortunately, Potiphar's wife also took an immediate liking to Joseph, who was extremely handsome. "Love me," she murmured in his ear one day.

"No, no," said Joseph. "Your husband has been kindness itself to me. How could I betray his trust?"

Potiphar's wife was not deterred. "Love me," she simpered, tugging at his beautiful Egyptian coat. Joseph took to his heels and ran. Potiphar's wife, her pride wounded, screamed, "Stop that man! He tried to kiss me! Filthy Israelite! Presumptuous boy!"

Potiphar, thinking himself betrayed by his most trusted servant, had Joseph thrown into prison, a forlorn, forgotten man in a foreign country. The jailer, however, took an immediate liking to Joseph, who could turn his hand to anything, and trusted him more and more with the running of the jail. Joseph never let him down. Shortly, two new prisoners arrived. One was Pharaoh's butler, one his baker. And both were troubled by dreams.

"I dreamt I was standing under a vine with three branches. I watched the grapes ripen, and crushed them into Pharaoh's cup."

"God has explained your dream to me," said Joseph. "In three days you will be pardoned and go back to work at the palace."

"Well, what about my dream then?" said the baker eagerly. "I dreamt I had three baskets of bread on my head, and the birds were eating out of the topmost basket. Does that mean I'll be free of here in three days, too?"

"I'm afraid so," said Joseph. "In three days Pharaoh will have you hanged, and the vultures will circle in the sky overhead."

Three days later it was the Pharaoh's birthday, and he was

sorely in need of his butler for the festivities. Choosing to overlook the man's crime, he ordered his release from prison. There was little time for farewells.

"Put in a good word for me, when you're standing beside Pharaoh's throne once more," said Joseph. "I've done nothing wrong, you see."

"Of course! Of course! How could I forget the man who read my dream?"

Other messengers came for the baker. "I suppose Pharaoh needs extra bread baked for his birthday feast," he said, jumping to his feet.

"No, just a good hanging to entertain the crowds," replied the soldiers.

The butler was so happy to be back at the palace that he shut out all thoughts of the prison. Joseph slipped his mind entirely, and for two more years lay in prison, a forlorn, forgotten man in a foreign country.

Then Pharaoh began to have dreams. He dreamt of the River Nile, that blue spine of his sand-yellow country. Seven fat cows came lumbering out of the water, followed by seven so thin that their ribs showed. Horn by hoof, the thin cows wolfed down the fat ones. He dreamt, too, of waving cornfields, of seven huge ears of corn bending the stalks under them. Alongside stood seven scrubby ears blasted to blackness, which battered down the seven good ears. "What does it mean? Won't someone tell me?" said Pharaoh, but none of his soothsayers could make sense of his dreams.

Something stirred in the butler's memory. "There's a young Hebrew in the prison who can do wonders with dreams," he ventured nervously.

Joseph was sent for, and Pharaoh took an immediate liking to him, for what he said made perfect sense. "The fat cows and heavy ears of corn are my God's promise of seven wonderful harvests. The thin cows and blighted corn are seven years of fam-

ine to follow. You'd best appoint a good man to take charge of storing the surplus, if your people are to survive the famine."

Pharaoh listened, his head resting on his hand. For a moment he was silent. Then he got up, tugged a ring off his finger and put it on Joseph's hand. "Do it," he said. "You shall be my voice in Egypt."

That is how Joseph came to be Chancellor of Egypt. Everything happened as he had said. The fertile black mud left behind by the Nile's annual flood produced harvests bigger than anyone could remember. Joseph had silos built in every city, where the surplus grain was stored like heaps of gold in treasure-houses. When the famine came, the Nile shrinking to a trickle, the silt drying to dust, the corn withering on the stalk, Joseph rationed the grain from the silos and the people still ate bread.

The famine spread far afield. Up in Canaan, Jacob and his eleven sons were hungry every day. "What are you waiting for?" Jacob scolded. "Get yourselves into Egypt and buy corn!" His youngest son, Benjamin, he kept at home, for since Joseph's disappearance, he set all his hopes on the boy.

• • •

Nothing escaped the ear of Egypt's Chancellor. Joseph was informed at once when his brothers entered Egypt. He sent for them – knew them instantly – but of course they did not recognize this grand Egyptian personage, eyelids stained with black kohl, hair cut in a heavy fringe, arms banded with gold. "I believe you are all spies," he told them, and threw them into prison. How they panicked! How they protested their innocence, pouring out details of family and home. Joseph appeared to relent, freeing all but Simeon. "You shall have your corn," he said. "But if you want more, and if you want this hostage to live, next time bring this '*youngest* brother' you speak of." When they had gone, Joseph walked his moonlit rooms, weeping out loud at the thought of the childhood lost to him.

Dazed and bewildered, the brothers stumbled home to Canaan. To add to their amazement, they found the money they had paid for the corn tied inside the sacks. They tried to explain to Jacob what had happened, but he was old, terrified, confused. "First Joseph! Now Simeon! Well, you shan't take Benjamin! No! It would be the death of me!" Only when the corn ran out did the brothers *have* to return to Egypt, and they dared not go without Benjamin.

When Joseph saw his little brother, he hid his face and cried until the kohl ran in dark lines down his Hebrew face. He treated

And Joseph gathered corn as the sand of the sea, very much, until he left numbering; for it was without number.
GENESIS 41:49

his brothers to a feast, seating them all in order of age (how did he know such things?) and filling Benjamin's plate five times over. But did he share his great secret? No. This time, when he sent them home, he had their sacks filled with corn, their money returned to them . . . and a silver cup hidden in the saddlebag of Benjamin's ass. No sooner had they left the city than he sent troops after them: "Stop! Thieving Hebrews! In the name of Pharaoh! You are under arrest!" Imagine their horror when the silver cup was found.

Trembling, protesting, staunchly defending their little brother, they were tumbled back into the presence of the Chancellor. "Bow down before the might of Egypt!" bellowed the guard, and they fell on their knees.

Just as the sheaves and the stars had done, in Joseph's dreams.

Then Joseph uttered a cry so loud that every soul in Pharaoh's palace heard it. "*Look at me!* Don't you know me? I am Joseph your brother! No, don't be afraid. You did me a service the day you sold me into slavery. You see? God has made me the Voice of Egypt. Go home and fetch our father. Bring him here. There are five more years of famine ahead, and we shall see them through together, as a family." And he kissed each brother as though they were the dearest and best kin a man ever had.

When Jacob's sons told him the news, he could not take it in at first. Joseph alive? Joseph Chancellor of Egypt? But God whispered in his ear – in a dream, as it happens: "Go down to Egypt, Jacob. Your tribe will grow to be a great nation while you're there. Don't be afraid. I shall go with you, and one day, one day, Jacob, I shall bring you all home again as well."

MOSES IN THE BULRUSHES

THE WHOLE of Joseph's family moved to Egypt and settled there and, with Joseph effectively running the country, they were both happy and welcome. They succeeded at everything they set their hands to, and had big, healthy families whom the Egyptians treated with respect. After Joseph died, all that changed. A new Pharaoh looked around him and saw almost as many Hebrew immigrants as Egyptians. "What if they ever rose up in revolt? They could take our own country away from us!"

So he gave orders for the Hebrews to be put to work like convicts, on hard and heavy work. He employed overseers with whips who forced them to make bricks and break rocks, to sweat and toil at building two huge cities for the Pharaoh's treasure. And so that they could never outnumber the Egyptians, Pharaoh commanded, "Drown every boychild born to a Hebrew!"

Give birth to a baby and see him murdered before her very eyes? One particular mother would as soon have taken the heart from her chest, the eyes from her face. So she kept her newly born son hidden until he was three months old. Her older boy, Aaron, (born in safer times) and daughter Miriam faithfully kept the secret, said not a word of the baby to friends or neighbours. But how can a baby be kept from crying? And such sounds carry in the dead of night.

Sooner than have her baby found and killed, the mother wove a basket out of reeds, daubed it with waterproof pitch, and laid her baby inside it. Then holding her daughter Miriam's hand so tightly that it hurt, she carried the basket down to the river.

The tall bulrushes stood like the wicks of a thousand candles, glowing in the low morning sun. She set the cradle afloat, and it

And Pharaoh charged all his people, saying, Every son that is born ye shall cast into the river, and every daughter ye shall save alive.

EXODUS 1:22

*And when she had
opened it, she saw
the child: and,
behold, the babe
wept. And she had
compassion on him,
and said, This is
one of the Hebrews'
children.*

EXODUS 2:6

bobbed against the rushes making them nod and sway. The mother ran home in tears. But Miriam stayed to see what would happen. Almost at once the sound of approaching voices drifted along the bank. Quickly, Miriam hid.

The Pharaoh's daughter and her maids were coming down to bathe. They waded into the river, their skirts spreading wide on the water. "Did you hear that?" said the Princess, holding up her hand. Her friends stopped splashing and listened. A baby was crying somewhere nearby. Then the Princes glimpsed the little tarry basket among the bulrushes, and when she lifted the lid, saw a little baby boy blinking in the bright light. "It's one of the Hebrews' babies," she whispered.

Hidden in the long grass, Miriam held her breath. Would the Princess fling her little brother out into deep water? That was the law, after all.

"He's beautiful," said the Princess, who had no children of her own. "I shall keep him."

"In that case you'll need someone to feed and nurse him!" exclaimed Miriam, darting out of her hiding-place. "I know just the person!"

"Let her come to the palace. I shall pay her a good wage," said the Princess, ". . . I believe I shall call him 'Moses', because it means 'lifted out', and I lifted him out of the water."

So Moses was reunited with his mother – she even earned money for looking after him! And Moses grew up like a member of the Egyptian royal family, wanting for nothing. He dressed, he spoke, he lived like an Egyptian . . . but beneath the fine linen and the circlets of gold, he remained Hebrew in heart and soul. His Hebrew mother made sure of that.

Did Pharaoh know where his new "grandson" had come from? How could he fail to? Did Pharaoh resent it, who so resented and feared all the other Hebrews in his kingdom? When Moses grew to manhood, he would have to tread very carefully indeed if he was to avoid the wrath of Pharaoh.

THE BURNING BUSH

MOSES, adopted by a princess of Egypt, grew up as an Egyptian prince. But since his true mother took care of him, she never let him forget that he was a Hebrew. "The one true God chose us Hebrews – us children of Abraham – for His special care and blessing. We are His Chosen People," she would say. But Moses saw no blessings fall on his fellow Israelites. He only saw how the immigrant Hebrews were being turned into labourers by the Egyptians, forced to do the hard, dirty work for next to nothing. Like donkeys they were flogged; like worn-out donkeys they bent and staggered under the strain.

One day, Moses saw an Egyptian foreman hitting a Hebrew worker without reason and without pity. The Hebrew blood in Moses' veins stirred, and he grabbed the bully round his thick neck and did not let go till the man fell dead at his feet. Quickly, guiltily, Moses looked round. Had anyone seen him? Surely the worker he had saved would say nothing? Moses scraped a hurried grave in the sand and rolled the dead body into it. No one need ever know. Who would miss such a man, after all?

Next day, he saw two Hebrew boys fighting each other, and remonstrated with them. "Hey! Is that any way for fellow Hebrews to behave?"

The brawling pair got up, spitting dirt. "What you going to do about it?" said one, surly and sneering. "Kill me, like you killed that Egyptian?"

So his crime was known! Moses had to leave, and quickly too, before Pharaoh got to hear of it! Not a moment too soon, he fled the country.

Stopping by a well to drink, he saw a group of girls being bullied by some shepherds – made to wait for their water till the men had finished. "I believe these girls were here first," said Moses, again defending the weak against the strong. The shepherds took one look at this richly dressed, commanding "Egyptian" and backed down, muttering and grumbling. Moses had made real friends of the girls, and it was with their father, Jethro, that he found a home, a bolt-hole, a refuge outside the borders of Egypt.

Meanwhile, things became worse and worse in Egypt. The old Pharaoh died, but the new one also looked on the immigrant Hebrews as nothing more than slaves. They never had enough food to eat, enough sleep to restore their broken spirits. They would have liked to leave, but Pharaoh needed his army of worker ants, his ghetto of labourers.

Moses' new life was happy by comparison, though it was no longer the life of a prince, only a shepherd grazing sheep on the slopes of Mount Horeb. He married one of Jethro's daughters, and had a son. Such things steady a man, make him prize home and safety, having a wife and child to think of. But one day something happened which obliged Moses to risk all his new-found happiness.

He was walking along a goat track on Mount Horeb when he saw a bush ablaze. Nothing so remarkable in that: all the vegetation was tinder-dry and grass fires happen. But as this bush burned, none of its leaves charred, none of its berries shrivelled, none of its twigs turned to ash.

Suddenly a voice spoke out of the bush: "Moses! Take off your sandals! This is holy ground." (Moses knew at once that he was in the presence of God, and covered his face with his sleeve.) "I have heard the cries of my people, slaving and dying in Egypt, and I mean to fetch them out and lead them to a land of their own – a land flowing with milk and honey. Go to Pharaoh and tell him: 'Let my people go'."

Moses was aghast. "Who, me?"

"I will be with you, I promise. Afterwards, you and I shall meet again on this mountain."

*Put off thy shoes
from off thy feet, for
the place where-
upon thou standest
is holy ground.*
EXODUS 3:5

*And I have said, I
will bring you up
out of the affliction
of Egypt . . . unto
a land flowing with
milk and honey.*
EXODUS 3:17

And God said unto Moses, I AM THAT I AM . . . Thus shalt thou say unto the children of Israel, I AM hath sent me unto you.

Moses began to panic. "But will even the *Hebrews* listen? I'll say to them, 'The God of your fathers has sent me to you!', and they'll say, 'Prove it. Who is He? What is His name?'"

"Tell them, then, that I am Yahweh – that's to say, I AM WHAT I AM. They will listen, Moses, and so will Pharaoh. He won't like it, but I shall make him listen."

"But . . . but . . . I'm not an eloquent man. I can't make speeches . . ."

"Moses . . ." The voice started to sound impatient. "Your brother Aaron is still living in Egypt. Take him with you, if you must. But after all, it will be my words you speak. The only weapon you will need is a shepherd's crook."

Moses did not need to seek out his brother. Aaron sensed that he was needed and stood waiting for Moses when he re-entered the borders of Egypt.

LET MY PEOPLE GO

"LET MY PEOPLE GO and worship – a religious holiday – just three days!" It was not an unreasonable request, but Pharaoh did nothing out of kindness.

"Why should I? And look – you and your brother have unsettled the brickmakers. They've all stopped working, to gossip. Overseer! Put them back to work. And tell them, no more straw. From now on, they can make bricks without straw!" (Do you know how hard it is to make bricks? How impossible to make them without straw to bind together the red mud?)

Moses was bewildered. All he had done was to make matters worse for the Hebrews. "Is this what you wanted, Lord?" he asked in his soul, despairingly.

"Prove it," said Pharaoh suddenly. "Prove your God worthy of all this *worship*." Moses and Aaron looked at one another and grinned. Aaron threw down his shepherd's crook on the stone palace floor. It flexed, coiled, peeled its bark and out slithered a smooth spotted snake!

"Huh!" said the supercilious Royal Magicians and hurled down their rods of office with a noise like tent poles collapsing. Suddenly the floor was alive with snakes. Fortunately, Aaron's snake ate all the others, but Pharaoh was no more impressed, for all that. Such *ordinary* magic!

So after that, the magic God worked was unprecedented, ferocious, awesome. *"Let my people go,"* said Moses, *"or the God I serve will plague you with plagues and torment you with suffering."*

But Pharaoh refused.

At the touch of the shepherd's crook, the water of the River Nile turned a thick glutinous red: the fish rolled over and died, the crops in the water-meadows choked, the canals, pools and

Thus saith the Lord God of the Hebrews, Let my people go, that they may serve me.
EXODUS 9:1

cisterns stank of blood. A woman pouring water into a basin dropped the jug in horror, as warm red blood slopped into the bowl.

But Pharaoh still refused Moses' request.

Next day, the vile Nile swarmed with frogs. They hopped into the houses, into cradles and beds, into dishes and pots, into the women's hair and the men's beer. The noise of them at night shredded the darkness, and frogspawn floated in jellied clumps in all the wells.

"Take away the frogs!" cried Pharaoh, and Moses did so. Within the day they lay about in a thousand soft green piles of slime, gathering flies. And rid of the frogs, Pharaoh felt free to refuse Moses' request.

So after the frogs came a plague of flies, rattling into the eyes and noses and mouths of the Egyptians like a thick black rain.

After the flies came a cattle sickness which wiped out all the Egyptian herds (but left the Israelite cows healthy). After the cattle disease came an epidemic of boils and sores, festering and itching, scarring the soft bodies of every Egyptian, though not one Israelite suffered.

After the boils came a hailstorm – great pebbles of ice shovelled out of the sky on to the heads of Egyptian men and Egyptian cattle, Egyptian flax and Egyptian trees. Thunder rampaged about the sky while sheets of lightning seemed to be burning down the walls of the world.

After the hail came locusts, stripping away every green leaf, smothering the entire landscape in a crackling blanket of brittle bodies, darkening the sky in their cloudy millions as they stripped the fields and gardens of Egypt bare. Every plague changed Pharaoh's mind. And the end of every plague saw him go back on his promise to let the Israelites leave.

After the locusts came darkness – a dark like being underground, a dark so absolute that it seemed the sun must have blown

out like a candle: a three-day blindness of Dark. The Egyptians
fumbled each other's faces, clung to each other's clothes, thinking
never to see again.

"All right! All right!" cried Pharaoh, peering through the dark
at the sound of Moses' voice. "The Hebrews shall have their
three days' worship . . . But tell them to leave their animals here,
so that I know they'll be back."

"They're our sacrificial animals – our burnt offerings," said
Moses reasonably. "We have to take them with us."

"Just get out of here and never let me see your face again!"
raged Pharaoh, missing the steps of his throne in the dark and
sitting down heavily. When returning daylight dazzled through
the window, he was quite alone.

But God had not finished with perfidious Pharaoh. He sent

just one more plague to punish his broken promises: the worst plague of all.

Moses instructed the Hebrews to stay home that night, stain their doorposts with blood, and bake bread quickly, for a journey. Then, in the small, terrible hours of darkest night, the Angel of Death visited Egypt and everyone living there. If, with his blazing eyes, he saw the mark of blood on the lintel, he passed over. But where he saw no blood, he went in – no lock can keep him out – and kissed the firstborn child of the house.

Hebrews call it the night of the Passover, and celebrate it each year with a feast. The Egyptians had no name to give such a night of grief. All life long they tried to *forget* that terrible night when their children died in their beds. From the Egyptian town, at first light, came a thousand cries of heartbreak, a noise that echoed between the white-faced pyramids in the Valley of the Kings. From the Israelite ghetto came not a sound – only the residual smell of baking bread. The Hebrews had gone – not for three days, but for ever, turning their backs on Egypt, following Moses.

But Pharaoh, holding the body of his oldest son in his arms, hardened his heart and curled his lips back off his teeth. *"Get them back!"* he told his generals. *"Fetch me back my slaves!"*

THE PARTING
OF THE RED SEA

HUNDREDS of chariots, thousands of foot soldiers streamed out of the city in pursuit of the Israelites. The caravan of refugees wound slowly through the countryside. Impeded by its old men and women, babes in arms, weary toddlers and lumbering animals, the progress it made was slow. But no one realized that the Egyptians were closing fast on them from the rear.

A column of smoke, like a twisting cyclone, sprang up out of the ground and moved ahead of the Israelites, leading the way. At night (when they could not have seen smoke) the column was of fire – the kind of holy fire which blazed in the burning bush. In this way, the freed slaves were guided on their way and, travelling night and day, reached the shores of the Red Sea: a narrow isthmus of water at that place, but a seemingly impassable obstacle, nevertheless.

By now, Pharaoh's army was within sight, raising its own column of dust, kicking up a sandstorm. "Is this what you brought us out of Egypt for?" the people wailed at Moses. "To be trapped against the sea and slaughtered like sheep?" But the column of smoke, like a huge genie, whirled around to the rear, and stood between Hebrew and Egyptian all day and all night.

In the morning, Moses stretched out that gnarled old shepherd's crook once more and – lo and behold! – the sea writhed. The waves started to quarrel, then draw apart like two warring armies. A corridor appeared – a path of dry land through the sea. The ocean had parted to let them through!

In went the Hebrews, gazing up at the glassy walls of water on either side.

In went the Egyptians, at Pharaoh's command, pounding

And the Lord said unto Moses . . . lift thou up thy rod, and stretch out thine hand over the sea, and divide it: and the children of Israel shall go on dry ground through the midst of the sea.
EXODUS 14:15, 16

after the runaways, drawing their swords, lifting their spears, whipping on their horses down the corridor of water.

When the last little Hebrew goat had trotted ashore on the other side of the narrow strait, Moses stretched out his staff again. And the walls of water folded themselves one over the other. The waves tumbled into one another's arms. The corridor through which the Hebrews had walked no longer existed, or if it did, was busy with caravans of coloured fish to-ing and fro-ing.

The Egyptians tried to turn back, but their chariot wheels were bogged down in the wet sand. The water closed over their heads like an eleventh plague more terrible than all the rest. The whole of Pharaoh's army was swallowed up by the Red Sea, and their chariot wheels still spin in the tides, and their weapons are still buried in the sea-bed sand.

Safe on the seashore, the Israelite women got out tambourines and little tinging cymbals, and danced to celebrate the majesty of God, and how He had troubled to take care of His Chosen People. Then they turned away from the sea to go on – and were confronted by waterless wilderness withering under a hot sun. The journey was not over. It had only just begun.

THE PARTING OF THE RED SEA

And the children of Israel went into the midst of the sea upon the dry ground: and the waters were a wall unto them on their right hand, and on their left.
EXODUS 14:22

The Lord is my strength and song, and he is become my salvation: he is my God, and I will prepare him an habitation; my father's God, and I will exalt him.
EXODUS 15:2

A GOLDEN CALF
FOR A GOD

ALL THEIR LIVES they had lived in Egypt, among Egyptian idols, Egyptian marvels, Egyptian traditions. Life had been hard, but people get used to anything in time, even slavery. Finding themselves suddenly in the desert and hardly even understanding how or why, the Israelites took fright. "We'll starve! Why did you bring us out here, Moses, to starve and see our children starve?"

Moses did not know how to answer them, but he knew to enquire of God.

And God sent manna to feed the children of Israel. It was there in the morning, like a white frost which melted in the heat of the sun. It could be gathered like seed and ground like grain, and it tasted of wafers made with honey. On the day before the Sabbath, there was twice as much: no one had to work on the holy Sabbath collecting it. The faith of the Israelites was renewed, their praise and gratitude was unlimited as the manna strewing the ground. Like manna it melted away in the sun.

"We'll die of thirst! Why did you bring us out here, Moses, to parch and see our children die of thirst?"

Moses did not know how to answer them, but he knew to enquire of God.

And God showed him the hill to climb, the exact place to strike with his shepherd's crook. Water streamed from the rock face in a pure, icy torrent, and the people splashed about in it, whooping with delight, drenching their dusty clothes till the colours showed bright once more.

"I am going up to the mountain to speak with God," said Moses. "I leave you in my brother's charge." And the people thrilled to think of their leader speaking with the One True God,

Then said the Lord unto Moses, Behold, I will rain bread from heaven for you . . .
EXODUS 16:4

bringing back word to them.

After Moses left for his rendezvous with God, Mount Sinai was convulsed with earthquakes, enveloped in smoke and darkness, as though a volcano were erupting. They waited for him to return, but Moses did not come back – not the next day or the day after that. When weeks passed and still he did not reappear, the people grew frightened, as sheep without a shepherd take fright. "What if Moses is dead? What if the smoke and the earthquake killed him? What if there was no God waiting for him up there? Give us a god we can understand, Aaron – one we can see

A GOLDEN CALF FOR A GOD

And Moses drew near unto the thick darkness where God was.
EXODUS 20:21

– a god like the ones the Egyptians have!" There was no reasoning with them.

Aaron (who was a lesser man than his brother) gave way. He let them melt down their jewellery and coins. He let them cast an idol like the gods worshipped in Egypt: strong, beautiful, terrible.

The code for living which God taught Moses on Mount Sinai was thorough and long. It took time to write down. Only the first ten of His Commandments are famous, remembered the world over, but God said much more, knowing how the Israelites loved detailed instructions, rules for every aspect of life. There on the mountain slopes, God dictated rules for living, while down in the valley, the children of Israel were busy breaking every one.

I am the Lord thy God . . .
Thou shalt have no other gods before me.
Thou shalt not make unto thee any graven image . . .
Thou shalt not take the name of the Lord thy God in vain . . .
Remember the sabbath day, to keep it holy.
Honour thy father and thy mother . . .
Thou shalt not kill.
Thou shalt not commit adultery.
Thou shalt not steal.
Thou shalt not bear false witness against thy neighbour.
Thou shalt not covet . . . any thing that is thy neighbour's.

EXODUS 20:2 17 IN PART

Then Moses stood in the gate of the camp, and said, Who is on the Lord's side? let him come unto me.

EXODUS 32:26

When Moses, burdened with two huge slabs of graven stone, walked out of the smoke, he saw below him a scene of pagan frenzy. The people were dancing and yelping, bowing down to a golden calf – a statue of the Egyptian bull-god, Apis – and festooning it with presents. They had already convinced themselves that a metal moulding they had cast themselves the day before was a real god capable of seeing and rewarding their worship.

Moses was so filled with rage at their ingratitude and disobedience, that he smashed the stone Commandments then and there. A dreadful punishment was meted out to those who had betrayed their one true God.

It was not everyone – not by any means. There were those who had not worshipped the golden calf and who were still hungry for God's laws. So for forty days Moses went back into the smoke, and when he returned he carried two new slabs of stone, the Commandments of God carved on them with hammer and chisel. His face shone, because he had spent so long in God's company.

They made a beautiful box called an ark for the Commandments, and carried it with them on their journey. And wherever they stopped, God's commands, in their Ark of the Covenant, stood at the centre of their worship. In those days of wandering, their temple was a tent, simply a big tent. But one day, they would reach a homeland where they could set down the Ark of the Covenant and house it in a temple befitting what it represented: that Almighty God had bent low enough to speak His wishes in the ears of humankind.

A GOLDEN CALF
FOR A GOD

Thus was all the work of the tabernacle of the tent of the congregation finished: and the children of Israel did according to all that the Lord commanded Moses, so did they.
EXODUS 39:32

BALAAM'S DONKEY

"IT CANNOT BE ALLOWED," said the haughty Balak, King of Moab. "If these Israelites think they can share our land of milk and honey, they can think again. I'll destroy them, or turn them back into the wilderness!" But before he made war, he took the usual steps to guarantee winning. He sent for Balaam, a diviner – a sort of wizard – the best man anywhere for delivering a curse. If Balaam blessed a man, that man prospered. If he cursed a man, he invariably suffered some dreadful disaster.

For all his strange profession, Balaam was an honest, God-fearing man, and was unwilling to deliver Balak's curse. But the King would not take no for an answer, so Balaam set off for the battlefront in Moab. The journey was long, and he rode his faithful old ass. All his life he had ridden her, come-here, go-there, and they were great friends.

Then, as the road narrowed between a vineyard and a wall, the donkey stopped dead. "Hup! Yah! Get on! Move!" Balaam's heels drummed the old ass's ribs. "Giddy up! Yeraah! Get on, you lazy object!" But the ass only took a few steps back. Balaam snapped a branch off the vine and thrashed her until dust flew out of her coat. "Gee up! Grrr! Shift yourself, you idle bag of bones!" But the donkey only trotted into the vines, leaving bunches of grapes dangling from Balaam's ears, then lunged the other way, squashing Balaam's foot against the wall.

That was when Balaam really lost his temper. He got off and started to thump the ass with his stick, yelling, hopping about, and shouting at her the kinds of things he was supposed to be shouting at the Israelites.

Suddenly, the ass furled her velvety lips off her yellow teeth

And when the ass saw the angel of the Lord, she fell down under Balaam: and Balaam's anger was kindled, and he smote the ass with a staff.

NUMBERS 22:27

and spoke: "What's that for? Haven't we been friends, man and donkey, all our lives? What's the matter with you? Why beat me? Do I normally behave like this?" Balaam gulped. "Do you seriously expect me to push past an angel with a drawn sword? Look at him, why don't you?"

Balaam put his hands over his eyes, then peered through his fingers. Sure enough, there in the narrow gap stood a huge, stocky warrior of an angel, wielding a lethal sword. "And about time too," said the angel. "Your donkey could see me from the start. I was just on the point of killing you to save her from your cruelty."

Balaam fell on his face alongside the ass. "I'll go back! I'll go back home! Honestly! I won't go and meet Balak. If that's what you want!"

"That is not . . ." said the angel, putting away his sword, "quite what God asks of you."

• • •

Next day, Balaam met with Balak as arranged. Balak took him to the top of a hill and pointed out the Israelite tents encamped below. "Curse them."

"I'll consult with God and do as He wishes. I can't say more."

"Yes, yes. Just do it," said Balak, and he mustered all the Moabite princes and generals to hear the Israelites roundly cursed.

Balaam went up to a high place. All faces turned towards him. *"King Balak sent for me to curse the Israelites. But how can I curse God's Chosen People? God brought them out of Egypt and there is no nation like them. Bless them and all their children. May they live and thrive for ever!"*

Balak turned purple with rage. "I sent for you to curse my enemies and you've blessed them!"

"I can only speak according to God's wishes. I did warn you. *May no magic ever work against them, nor no spells ever be cast upon . . .*"

"All right! All right!" said Balak urgently. "Don't curse them, if that's how you feel, but don't bless them either!"

"I can only speak according to God's wishes," said Balaam, and went on to bless the Israelites till his blessings filled the sky like an arkful of doves, and his donkey brayed so loud with laughter that the Israelites in their tents must have heard her.

BLOWING DOWN JERICHO

BEFORE the Israelites escaped slavery in Egypt and walked out into the desert, God had promised them a land of their own to go to – a land of milk and honey. Forty years later, they at last saw that land laid out before them, beyond the River Jordan. Moses sent spies over the river, one of them a man called Joshua who came back singing the praises of this fertile land, this Canaan.

Moses, though he lived long enough to see Jordan, was not destined to cross over it. On the day he died, he laid his old hands in blessing on Joshua and said, "You are their leader now."

For thirty days the Israelites mourned the death of Moses. Then on the thirty-first morning, they woke up, went out to gather the miraculous manna which had kept them from starvation in the wilderness, and found it had . . . disappeared! If God's Chosen People were to eat now, it would have to be from the orchards and fields on the other side of Jordan.

But it was no empty paradise awaiting them over there, no Garden of Eden with the gates left ajar. There were people living there already, in fortified towns and with great armies ready to defend the land. What the Chosen People faced now was a time of war.

The very first place they came to was Jericho, a dour city, spiny with palm trees, sunk deep in the belly of the earth. When its people saw the Israelites trooping towards their city, they shut up the gates and prepared for a siege. Joshua stood wondering what Moses would have done to capture the city, as he studied the immense, forbidding walls. Out of the corner of his eye, he glimpsed a man with a drawn sword, and quickly drew his own. "Who goes there? Friend or foe?"

*BLOWING DOWN
JERICHO*

"Captain of your army and of Heaven's," said the stranger, "come with your battle orders. Listen well, Joshua, for this is how you shall take Jericho." Joshua fell on his face in reverent respect, and listened intently. But what strange battle plans they were!

Next day Joshua assembled a procession. The fighting men led, and behind them came seven priests with huge, curling rams'-horn trumpets. Behind them came the Ark of the Covenant holding the precious slabs on which God Himself had written His Laws. Behind the Ark walked everyone else — old men, women and children. Somewhere a drum set up the beat, and the column began to move. Round the city they marched, in one complete circle, and though the archers on the ramparts fired, their arrows fell short.

Next day, they did the same thing. For six days they circled Jericho once, at noon. By now the citizens stood jeering on the parapets: "Is that the best you can do? Too scared to attack?"

On the seventh day, they made not one but seven circuits of the city, the seven priests blew their seven rams'-horn trumpets

*And it came to pass
on the seventh day,
that they rose early
about the dawning
of the day, and
compassed the city
. . . seven times.
And it came to pass
at the seventh time,
when the priests blew
with the trumpets,
Joshua said unto
the people, Shout;
for the Lord hath
given you the city.*

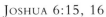
JOSHUA 6:15, 16

seven times — a strident racket that rampaged about the valley like the roar of wild beasts. At the sound of the trumpets, Joshua yelled to his people, "Now shout! Shout with joy! Shout with praise! *Shout out loud!*" The thousand braying cheers echoed off the rocky bluffs and the high city walls.

Like blood, the mortar between the boulders of the city wall began to run. The boulders themselves began to writhe and heave and grind together. The walls of Jericho fell as suddenly and simply as a tent collapsing, and the army of Israel simply walked through the rubble and into the city. Soon Jericho, felled by noise, lay as silent as death.

News of Joshua's coming, like the shockwave of an earthquake, travelled to every corner of the Promised Land. Rumour spoke of hailstorms battering to death whole armies of his enemies, of the sun and moon standing still in the sky to grant Joshua time for yet another victory.

For a season, the Land of Milk and Honey ran with blood.

GIDEON AGAINST THE ODDS

A LAND OF MILK AND HONEY, God had called Canaan, and it was true. The country was fertile and green, and the Israelites found everything they needed. They also found things they did not need: the cult of Baal, for instance. Forgetting God's Commandments and forgetting the debt they owed to the God of Israel, some began to worship this god-with-a-face, whose idols littered the countryside, set about with sacred groves of trees.

Like a punishment for disobedience, the Midianites came. They did not want conquest or revenge, or to drive their new neighbours out of Canaan. They raided at harvest-time, and pillaged and stripped the land as bare as a plague of locusts.

God sent an angel to Gideon, son of Joash. "Cast down Baal, then cast out the Midianites," said the angel.

Now Gideon was only young and no natural-born hero. "I'm a farmer, not a general . . . Besides, how do I know God sent you?"

"Put down that basket of food," said the messenger, and, striking it with his staff set it on fire.

"I believe you! I'll do it!" said Gideon. But then the messenger was gone, and Gideon wondered if the whole thing had not been a trick. "Give me a sign, Lord, and I'll do it." He laid a sheep's fleece on the ground. "If that's wet in the morning, I'll know."

In the morning the ground was dry, but the fleece so sodden Gideon could hardly lift it. "Don't be angry, Lord, but could you do it the other way round? Then I'd really know." Next morning the ground was slippery silver with dew, the fleece fluffy and dry. Gideon had run out of excuses. It was hardly surprising, though, that Gideon took such convincing. His own father, Joash, worshipped Baal.

The Lord is with thee, thou mighty man of valour.
JUDGES 6:12

Behold, I will put a fleece of wool in the floor; and if the dew be on the fleece only, and it be dry upon all the earth beside, then shall I know that thou wilt save Israel by mine hand, as thou hast said.
JUDGES 6:37

Now Gideon took ten men, in secret, at night, and vandalized his father's shrine to Baal, hacking down its sacred trees. But the outraged worshippers had no difficulty in tracking down the culprit, and when they did, they wanted Gideon put to death for what he had done.

Amazingly, Joash looked into his heart and found he loved and admired his son more than Baal or Baal's shrine. "If Baal feels offended let him punish my son himself. If he can't . . . I think I might just put my trust in Gideon's God and the God of our forefathers," said Joash fearlessly.

So Gideon lived to muster an army. But it was not much of an army, heaven knows: maybe five thousand men to fight the Midianite hordes. And half of them looked too frightened to fight.

"Not enough," thought Gideon, but he was answered by God's own voice.

"Too many. It is I who will win you this victory, Gideon, not strength of numbers."

So Gideon addressed his rag-tag army. "If any one of you is scared to fight, go now. No one will think any the worse of you."

They believed him. First in ones and twos, then in droves, they left. Two out of every three men went home.

"Not enough," thought Gideon, trying to count those left.

"Too many," said God. "Next time they drink, choose only the ones who lap from their cupped hands."

"Three hundred," said Gideon, scanning the river bank as his army drank – most of then kneeling to drink the water straight from the river. "Three hundred men to defeat the Midianite hordes."

"It's enough," said God.

On the night before the attack, Gideon went spying through the Midianite camp. Crawling between the black tents, he heard them whisper of nightmares and bad omens.

"I dreamt that this little barley loaf came rolling down the

By the three hundred men that lapped will I save you, and deliver the Midianites into thine hand . . .

JUDGES 7:7

mountain towards us and knocked down our tent."

"It's Gideon, that loaf," his companion replied. "He's going to win, I tell you. I feel it. It's destiny." They were scared. Why they should be, Gideon could not fathom, but the Midianites were scared of him . . . and a scared enemy is halfway to being beaten.

He played on those fears. He gave each of his men a pottery jar, a torch and a ram's-horn trumpet. Then he sent them in on three flanks. The torch-flames were hidden inside the pottery jars, so that the three hundred crept close without being seen. Then, at a signal, each man blew his trumpet, smashed the pot and loosed a banner of fire on to the night sky, shouting, "A sword for the Lord and for Gideon!"

It was a rout. The Midianites, in their panic and confusion, killed each other rather than the Israelites. Then they took to their heels and fled, swarming away like a plague of fat locusts, never to return.

SAMSON AND DELILAH

FOR MANY generations, the greatest enemies of the Israelites in the Promised Land were the warlike Philistines. It seemed, when Samson was born, that he was God's weapon to defeat them, for he had the strength of twenty men and great daring. But for all Samson hated the Philistine tribe, its women held a peculiar fascination for him. They do say love is akin to hate. He loved Delilah, a passionate, dark-eyed woman, and a Philistine to the core of her being.

"What is it that makes you so strong?" she asked Samson sweetly one night.

"Oh, that's one secret I must keep to myself," he answered. "It would never do for the Philistines to find out."

But Delilah would not be fobbed off. She had a pressing need to know. For she was a spy in the pay of her government, and armed men were hiding in the next room ready to seize Samson. So she pouted and teased, cajoled and cuddled him, until Samson rocked his big head on his shoulders and laughed too. "Oh, very well. If you were to tie me up in arrowstrings, I'd be as weak as the next man. Now you know all the secret there is to know," he told her.

Delilah kissed him and waited for him to fall asleep. Then she wound him and bound him in a spider's web of arrowstrings. Leaning over him she hissed in his ear, "Wake up, Samson! Philistines are attacking!" The men in the next room slid out from under the furniture.

Stretching himself as he woke, Samson broke every arrowstring. The strands fell round his feet like cut hair.

"Oh, Samson! You were teasing me!" cried Delilah. The men in the next room scurried back into hiding. "Don't you trust even me? Your own love?" Then Delilah sulked and sorrowed, flirted and frowned until she wore Samson down.

"Oh, very well. If you were to tie me up with brand-new ropes, I'd be as weak as the next man. Now you know," he told her.

Delilah clapped her hands delightedly, kissed him and waited for him to fall asleep. Then she wound him and bound him in a ship's rigging of brand-new ropes. Leaning over him, she hissed in his ear, "Wake up Samson! The Philistines are just outside!" The men in the next room drew their swords.

With one twist of his body, like a fish breaking from the hook, Samson snapped the ropes binding him; they fell in cords and twists round his feet, like cut hair.

"Oh, Samson, you lied to me!" cried Delilah, and the men in the next room scampered back into hiding. "How could you! You don't love me at all, or you wouldn't tell me such lies!" Then she wept and wailed, groaned and grieved. "You really don't love me at all!"

"Oh, but I do! Stop crying. I can't bear it when you cry. My secret's nothing very magical. My strength is in my hair, that's all. It's never been cut. Not since I was born. Cut it, and I'd be as weak as the next man!"

If I be shaven, then my strength will go from me, and I shall become weak, and be like any other man.

JUDGES 16:17

Delilah dried her tears. She took Samson's head on her lap and stroked his mane of hair till he fell sound asleep. And when he woke, there were scissors in Delilah's hands, Philistine swords at his throat and a shearing of dark hair on the bedroom floor. Samson had not even the strength to shield his eyes, or stop the Philistines blinding him or binding him or setting him to work like a donkey, at a treadmill.

The mill wheel turned. So did the year. The feast of Dagon came round – a pagan festival dear to the pagan Philistines. A great banquet was prepared. And what better entertainment for the lords and ladies of the land, than to see their old enemy Samson

*And Samson called
unto the Lord, and
said, O Lord God,
remember me, I
pray thee, and
strengthen me . . .
that I may be at
once avenged of the
Philistines . . .*
JUDGES 16:28

brought out in chains, like a dancing bear, and made to cavort for their pleasure.

They chained him between two great pillars in the centre of the room. They spat in his blind eyes. They kicked at his manacled ankles. But no one noticed – not even Delilah, his faithless lover – how Samson's hair had *grown down* in prison.

"Oh God!" he cried, though his lips did not move. "Lend me my strength one last time, and let me be revenged on the enemies of Your People! Let me die in doing it!"

Then he pushed against the pillars, his two hands whitening against the stone, the blood vessels swelling in his neck, the blood pumping through his heart. With a trickle of mortar, the bricks began to stir. Amid an avalanche of masonry, a rain of dust, a skyful of rubble, the great banqueting hall of the Philistines fell on to the greatest and best of the nation – three thousand enemies of Israel – three thousand and one souls silenced by the crash of a falling building. In his death, Samson killed more Philistines than in all the daring actions of his life.

Alongside him lay the carved idol called Dagon, smashed, reduced to a clutter of rubble. Its flower garlands were torn into curls and coils on the floor, like cut hair.

RUTH IN A FOREIGN LAND

REAL HUNGER is one of the few things which will make a man leave his birthplace and travel to a foreign country. Foreigners are so often disliked, mistreated. Famine drove the Israelite Elimelech to take his wife Naomi and two sons abroad. There, his sons married local girls. But tragedy followed disaster: first Elimelech died, then both his sons. Naomi was left desolate in a foreign country. She said to her daughters-in-law: "There's nothing to keep me here. I'm going home to Bethlehem. You go back to your parents' homes. You're both still young and pretty. You're sure to marry again."

Orpah sadly agreed it was for the best, kissed Naomi goodbye, and went home. But Ruth said, "No, Mother-in-law. I love you as dearly as my own mother. Where you go, I will go and where you make your home, that will be my home, too." It was an amazing act of love – to go into a foreign land with a penniless widow. In all probability, Ruth would never marry again, but live hand to mouth, despised by strangers, looking after her mother-in-law until the day she died.

Indeed, once they reached Bethlehem, their only means of eating was for Ruth to glean fallen grain from among the stubble at harvest-time. It was back-breaking work, leaning over in the hot sun to pick up single grains from between needle-sharp cut stalks – like picking fleas from a hedgehog. But Ruth never rested or paused. From dawn till dusk, she filled her pinafore with the litter of harvest, knowing that otherwise Naomi would go hungry.

That evening, Boaz, the owner of the field, passed by. "Who is that girl gleaning? I don't know her, do I?"

"A foreigner," he was told. "Came home with old Naomi. Devoted to her, so they say. Certainly doesn't mind hard work."

And Ruth said, Intreat me not to leave thee, or to return from following after thee: for whither thou goest, I will go; and where thou lodgest, I will lodge: thy people shall be my people, and thy God my God: Where thou diest, will I die, and there will I be buried: the Lord do so to me, and more also, if ought but death part thee and me.
RUTH 1:16, 17

Now it so happened that Boaz was a cousin of Naomi's. He was touched that a foreign girl should expend such tenderness on the old lady. "Tell the reapers to be a little more careless with their scythes," said Boaz, "and let a bit extra fall in her path."

So Ruth went home with her apron bulging, and astonished Naomi with how much grain she had gathered. "Boaz is a good man," the old lady observed shrewdly. "Do as I tell you, and all may still turn out better than I ever hoped."

That night, Boaz worked late on the threshing floor, thrashing the loose barley with a leather flail till the air was smoky with dust and swarming with husks. Ruth watched him at work – a man past his prime, but a good face, a kind face, a noble face. She did not speak, but watched from a shadowy corner, still as a harvest mouse. Boaz laid down his flail at last and ate a meal, washing the dust out of his throat with a flagon of wine. Still Ruth did not speak, but watched from a shadowy corner, still as a harvest mouse. Boaz lay down, exhausted, to sleep in the barn, as was his practice during the busy harvest season. He fell deep asleep. That was when Ruth went and uncovered his feet and lay down across them, as a dog sleeps at the feet of a beloved master. When Boaz stirred and found a strange woman at his feet he was completely unnerved. "What are you doing here?!"

"Naomi sent me," said Ruth. "She said I should say this: 'Cover your handmaiden with your cloak and let her sleep beside you.'" It was tantamount to a proposal of marriage!

Boaz was flabbergasted. "You're a very beautiful girl, Ruth! You could marry a man much younger and more handsome than me! I know how you've looked after my cousin Naomi – how much you've given up for her sake. You will always have my protection and friendship, you know that. But you don't want to marry an old man like me!"

"Cover your handmaiden with your cloak and let her sleep beside you," said Ruth, looking back at him steadily with her large, dark, Moabite eyes.

Boaz had thought his life nearly over, his days harvested and stored away. But he married Ruth and she gleaned such joy for him that they fed on love and happiness for many years to come. They had a son, too, a son who would never have been born but for one girl's kindness to a foreigner in Moab, one man's kindness to a foreigner in Bethlehem.

Nothing so very remarkable, even so, you might say. A chance meeting. A marriage. Nothing remarkable – except that their son's grandson was destined to be the greatest king in the history of Israel. Without their meeting, King David would not have been born.

SAMUEL! SAMUEL!

THERE WAS ONCE a woman who longed so for a child that she prayed, "Grant me a son, Lord, and I will give him back into Your service." True to her word, when a baby was born to her, she sent him, as soon as he could walk, to train as a priest. Old Eli had charge of Samuel's education. He saw real goodness in the boy's sweet face – though it was almost the last thing he did see: Eli was going blind.

At night, the two of them – priest and apprentice – would bed down in separate corners of the temple. One night, Samuel was woken just before dawn by a voice calling, "Samuel!" He ran to Eli's side, "Yes? What do you want?"

"I didn't call," said Eli, fuddled with sleep. "Go back to bed."

So Samuel lay down again, close by the Ark of the Covenant. But the voice called again: "Samuel!" He ran back to Eli.

The old man was irritated to be woken a second time. "I tell you I *didn't* call. Now go back to sleep."

A third time the voice called: *"Samuel! Samuel!"*

"But you *did* call me! I heard you!" the little boy insisted, shaking the sleeping priest by the shoulder.

Then Eli woke up to what was really happening. "Next time, you must say, 'Speak Lord. I'm listening.' "

The lamp guttered which burns all night in the temple. *"Samuel!"*

Samuel knelt up amid his blankets. "Speak, Lord. I'm listening." Then the voice of God spoke of a great grief coming to Eli. The news was so bad, that Samuel did not want even to repeat it to Eli. But next morning, when the old man asked him what God had said, the truth spilled out of Samuel.

"He says that your two sons are wicked, and not fit to take your place as priests when you die. He says that they shall both

And the Lord came, and stood, and called as at other times, Samuel, Samuel. Then Samuel answered, Speak; for thy servant heareth. And the Lord said to Samuel, Behold, I will do a thing in Israel, at which both the ears of every one that heareth it shall tingle.

1 SAMUEL 3:10, 11

die – that no one in your whole family will live to old age . . . Oh, Eli, I'm so sorry!"

But the old man, though he was heartbroken at the news, had long since realized the worthlessness of his two boys. He bowed his head, and as tears squeezed between his white lashes, said, "God is good. Let Him do as He sees fit." And in a way he was grateful to God that little Samuel had been there to break the dreadful news. His sons might not serve God in the Temple as High Priests, but Samuel would. The boy was too little to know it, but God had plainly chosen him to be a mighty prophet and priest.

THE THEFT OF THE ARK

And when the ark of the covenant of the Lord came into the camp, all Israel shouted with a great shout, so that the earth rang again.
1 SAMUEL 4:5

BY THE TIME Samuel had grown to manhood, war with the Philistines again ravaged the land of milk and honey. The Philistines, whom Samson had died to defeat, were growing in numbers and military strength once more. And they resented the Israelites occupying a land they considered theirs.

As the might of the Philistine army grew, it was decided that the Ark of the Covenant should be taken out of safekeeping, to lift the spirits of Israel's fighting men. Just then, its permanent home was at Shiloh, with old Eli its guardian. He stood by as it was carried away, with the same anxious grief that a parent feels, watching a child leave home. That Ark was the very soul of the Israelites, the heart of their religion. The merest sight of it made them shout aloud with joy, and filled them with fire.

And the Philistines knew it. So they fixed their sights on the Ark. When next they attacked, they went after the Ark itself and, amid carnage and terrible slaughter, carried it off to their own holy city of Ashdod. It was a rich prize – like ripping the heart out of their enemy.

"Rabbi! Master! Dreadful news!" panted the soldier on the steps of the temple at Shiloh. He was still bloodstained from battle, and sank down with exhaustion at Eli's feet. "The Philistines have defeated us! They've captured the Ark! It's gone!"

Eli said nothing. The news struck him like an arrow. It pierced his heart, and he died, then and there, with a cry of despair.

Meanwhile, the Ark was unceremoniously trundled into the temple in Ashdod. No thunderbolt struck down the Philistine thieves for the blasphemy of touching it. No wrathful Israelite God roared at them out of Heaven. They gloated and left the ornate chest as a tribute at the feet of their god, Dagon.

In the morning, Dagon was found lying on his face. They propped him up again and polished the gold from which he was carved, and thought no more about it. But in the night, Dagon fell with a crash which snapped his head from its neck, his hands from their stiff, metallic arms. A rat ran between the pieces of the broken idol.

But next day, the Philistines were barely able to shed a tear on Dagon's behalf. For their own bodies were wracked with suffering. An epidemic of boils smothered them in misery, paining them so much that they could barely wag a stick at the infestation of rats swarming through their houses and barns. They had thought to gain power over their enemies by seizing their shrine, but it seemed as if the God of Israel was not confined within that shrine nor shackled by any chains.

THE THEFT OF
THE ARK

And when they arose early on the morrow morning, behold, Dagon was fallen upon his face to the ground before the ark of the Lord; and . . . only the stump of Dagon was left to him.

1 SAMUEL 5:4

• • •

In the fields of Canaan, weary, unhappy Israelites reaped and stooked their harvest. Life must go on, even in wartime, even in the wake of disaster and loss. One reaper looked up and saw an ox cart trundling towards him pulled briskly along by two young oxen. There was no driver, and the oxen were too young to be properly broken in, and yet the cart came straight on down the road, its cargo rattling gaily in the back. The cart was carrying the Ark of the Covenant and a large pot of gold. The Philistines, urged to it by their priests and magicians, had sent back their booty, and with it a peace offering from a deeply disheartened people.

DAVID AND GOLIATH

SAMUEL was more than just a priest and a prophet. In those days, the priests ruled the nation, passing on God's instructions to the people. But one day they said to him, "Give us a king! Other nations have kings – give us a king!"

"You're making a mistake," said Samuel, but chose as good a man as he could find and anointed him King of Israel. He chose Saul. But though Saul was a fine warrior, he had faults – pride and envy – which grew larger with kingship. He suffered bouts of mental illness too – terrible depressions in which his temper was like thin ice waiting to break if anyone so much as came near.

So God whispered in Samuel's ear that he should anoint another king – secretly – to take Saul's place in due course. There was a wonderfully devout old man Samuel knew of, with a wealth of sons, and to him Samuel went in search of a candidate. He asked to meet all the sons, one by one. One by one, from oldest to youngest, they passed in front of the old priest. But none struck Samuel as the stuff of kings. "Have you no more sons, Jesse?" he asked the old man.

"Only David, my youngest. He's out looking after the sheep."

"Send for him," said Samuel. And no sooner did he see the boy – small, fresh-faced, ragged in shepherd's clothes and sandals, and grimy from his work, than he felt the approval of God filling the room saying, *"This is the one."* So Samuel poured a blessing of oil over the child's head, and swore the family to secrecy. The blessing was so unexpected and over so quickly, that David probably forgot all about it. Besides, there were things happening which seemed far more important.

The Philistines were attacking and, despite Saul's best efforts, it seemed they might sweep through the ranks of the Israelites

like fire through a forest. Several of David's brothers left home to
serve in Saul's army.

had a way about him. "You're not afraid?"

"No more than I was of the lions that attacked my sheep. I put a stop to them, with God's help."

There was no denying the boy's courage – or foolishness. "Take my sword and armour," said King Saul.

"I don't think I could stand up in your armour, and I really only need my sling," David replied politely.

"A *sling*? You can kill a man with a slingshot?"

"I don't know, but I killed the lions and the bears."

Saul threw up his hands in bewilderment. That the nation's freedom should depend on a little boy with a catapult! But David went out to fight Goliath, even so, wearing his shepherd's sheepskin waistcoat and pausing only to gather a handful of round pebbles from the bed of a stream.

Encased in heavy armour, like a giant turtle, and armed with a spear as thick as a tree, Goliath came out to meet his opponent. When he saw David, he was incensed at the insult. "Send a boy to fight *ME*?! I'll feed his eyes to the birds and his flesh to the wild beasts!" His massive sword slashed the air to shreds.

"But I shall kill you," was David's reply.

Like some grotesque pagan idol cast all in bronze, the armoured giant stamped remorselessly closer and closer. David slipped a stone into his leather sling and whirled it round his head. Once, twice, three times, he whirled the sling, then loosed the stone inside it. Flying too fast to be seen, the pebble hurtled through the dusty air – and struck Goliath between the eyes, making a wound like a third eye. For a moment he looked at David – a three-eyed ogre from a child's nightmare. Then he reeled once and, without loosening his grip on sword or spear, toppled forwards with a crash like a felled tree.

A gasp of disbelief from the Philistine army was swept away by the cheer which went up from the Israelites. "You have saved us from slavery!" cried Saul. "From today you shan't leave my side!"

DAVID AND
GOLIATH

The Lord that delivered me out of the paw of the lion, and out of the paw of the bear, he will deliver me out of the hand of this Philistine. And Saul said unto David, Go, and the Lord be with thee.
1 SAMUEL 17:37

Then said David to the Philistine, Thou comest to me with a sword, and with a spear, and with a shield: but I come to thee in the name of the Lord . . .
1 SAMUEL 17:45

And David did not. He was welcome among the King's retinue, not least because of his skill with the harp. When Saul's depressions came on him, like bleak weather, David would play to him and he would be soothed, a little soothed. A huge affection grew up between Saul and David. But more between David and Saul's son, Jonathan. Theirs was the kind of friendship made only once in a lifetime, and on it David's life depended. Things might have been very different had Saul known of Samuel's visit to the house of Jesse, of the oil blessing, of God's intention to make David the greatest king of all.

KING DAVID

DAVID AND JONATHAN were inseparable. The Prince gave David his clothes, his armour, his sword, and together they fought the Philistines till victory was theirs. But as the conquering armies marched home, the women streamed out of every city singing and dancing. "Saul has killed thousands, David tens of thousands!"

The songs irked Saul, preyed on his mind. He began to resent David, then to hate him with a livid jealousy. When his dark depression came down on him, like winter weather, his thoughts would centre all on David, and he would brood in sullen silence. One day, while David was playing the harp to soothe him, Saul suddenly picked up a spear and flung it at David. If he had not dived aside, it would have impaled him to the wall. He fled, without stopping to ask what he had done wrong. "Does he truly hate me enough to want me dead?" he asked Jonathan, and Jonathan was distraught that such a cloud should overshadow their friendship.

"Hide yourself behind the rocks at the end of the field where I practise archery. I'll sound out my father's state of mind, and tomorrow, if everything's all right, I'll shoot to one side of the rocks. If he truly means you harm, I'll shoot over your head and you will know to run, far and fast, beyond reach of Father and his spies . . . Only swear to me, if we never see each other again, never to stop loving me. No one's dearer to me than you, my friend."

So David hid behind the rocks on the archery field and waited. The arrows from Jonathan's bow flew far over his head, and plunged into the grass – though it seemed to Jonathan and David that each arrow pierced their hearts, for they would never meet again.

From that day onwards, Saul's hatred of David cankered into

an obsession. He pursued him pitilessly, hunted him like a wild beast. David had followers of his own, and cunning enough to outwit Saul. But he felt nothing but sad affection towards the old king. Once, when Saul was sitting in a cave, David and his troops surrounded the cave: they could have put an end to him then and there. But David would not see the King harmed. He crept up behind him, and sliced a length of braid from Saul's cloak. All unaware, Saul left the cave, but David emerged into the sunlight too, and called after him: "My Lord King!" Saul spun round, his sword half drawn. But David only held up the piece of cloak. "I could have killed you back there, but I have no wish to lift a finger against my rightful master."

Unfortunately, pity only drove Saul deeper and deeper into the dark. Everyone he wronged in his madness deserted him and joined the ranks of David, so that David's army grew and Saul's shrank. Out-and-out war between them was inevitable. David found himself in league with the Philistines, while Saul, demented with misgivings, torn between love and hatred for David, could no longer face the uncertain future. Contrary to all the laws of his religion, he visited a medium, the Witch of Endor. He went in disguise, but she knew him. He asked to speak with the spirit of dead Samuel, but the ghost which the medium conjured seemed to rise unwillingly. "Why do you disturb me, Saul?"

"Tomorrow I fight the Philistines. I must know. Will I win?"

"God will give Israel to the Philistines," came the reply, "and you and your sons will be spirits, like me, tomorrow evening."

So it happened, just as the ghost had said – perhaps *because* of what the ghost had said. Empty of hope and full of fear, Saul died in battle next day, alongside three of his sons.

The runner who brought David the news thought he would be pleased. But he tore his clothes in shreds and wept. "That the world's great ones should come to this! . . . And Jonathan? What of Prince Jonathan?"

"Dead, my lord," came the reply.

Then David sobbed out loud at the loss of his dearest friend. "Oh Jonathan! Jonathan! I love you dearer than a brother! And what love you showed me! That I should live to lose you like this!"

Even so, with Saul dead, David was soon chosen King of Israel. He was not a perfect man by any means – wilful and passionate, impetuous and just as inclined to sin as any of his subjects. But he believed absolutely in the power of God and in the nation of Israel. All the tribes of Israel flocked to him. Undivided, behind God's chosen man, they swept to victory after victory, their ultimate achievement the capture of the great city of Jerusalem.

I am distressed for thee, my brother Jonathan: very pleasant hast thou been unto me: thy love to me was wonderful, passing the love of women. How are the mighty fallen, and the weapons of war perished!

2 SAMUEL 1:26, 27

For generations, the Laws given by God to Moses had been carried about in the Ark of the Covenant, wherever the people wandered: through wars, famines, good and ill. Here at last was a city where the Israelites could set down their priceless burden, and build over it a temple befitting its holiness. For generations, the people had worshipped God in a tent, at altars scrabbled together out of rocks, in the flyblown desert, in the chaos of war. Now at last they could build a permanent temple, a place of silence and beauty, a home of learning and debate, a place comfortable with cool shadows, holy stillness and the wisdom of old men.

As David led the procession into Jerusalem, ahead of the Ark of the Covenant, he danced and sang for all he was worth.

KING SOLOMON THE WISE

IT WAS SOLOMON, David's son, who built the Temple in Jerusalem. David's embattled life had finally brought peace to Israel, and there was time and money to lavish on such projects. God was the architect, Solomon the overseer. Together they built the loveliest building in the world. For Solomon had the soul of a poet and the mind of a visionary. "I have built you a great house, Lord, where you may live for ever!" he declared, when the work was done.

He was like his father in many ways. They were both poets, both faithful servants of God. But Solomon was wiser by far. He was the wisest king ever to rule Israel. People travelled from far and near to drink in his words. And yet his was not a coldly scientific knowledge, it was an understanding of the human heart.

Take the time two women laid claim to the same baby. The child of one of the women had died, and she had stolen another woman's baby in its place. But which woman had done the stealing?

"This child's mine: yours is the dead one!" shrieked one.

"No! You stole mine when yours died!" the other retaliated. "While I was sleeping! You left your dead baby beside me and took mine! Do you think I'm a complete fool that I don't know my own boy?"

"I know you're clever enough to think up a filthy lie!" And they argued and fought while the baby wailed with distress at their feet, brandishing tiny clenched fists.

Solomon watched them, his chin on his hand, sadly shaking his head. "There's a simple solution," he said. "Cut the child in two and give a half to each. Fetch a sword!" The sword was brought: its curved glittering blade reflected the baby's pretty face.

I am but a little child: I know not how to go out or come in. Give therefore thy servant an understanding heart to judge thy people, that I may discern between good and bad . . .
1 KINGS 3:7, 9

And the king said, Divide the living child in two, and give half to the one, and half to the other.
1 KINGS 3:25

"Do it! At least she shan't have it!" ranted one mother. The blade of the sword was raised.

"No! Very well! He's hers! Don't kill him! Don't!" cried the other woman, falling to her knees.

Solomon rose from his throne and held her up. "The baby is yours," he said. "No parent could see her own child cut in two. You are plainly the true mother."

The Queen of Sheba, far away in Arabia, heard rumours of this wise judgement and many others, and travelled with all her retinue to Jerusalem, laden with gifts of precious spices, gold and jewels, to meet this wisest of kings. She asked Solomon about

every aspect of life, and he answered her every time more fully than she had ever hoped. "How did you become so wise?" she wanted to know.

"I dreamed that God offered me a reward for loyal service to my father," replied Solomon. "I asked for that greatest of blessings, wisdom. He liked my choice – granted my request and, because I had chosen wisdom, gave me all the other things I might have asked for – wealth, long life, the respect of my enemies."

"Not everyone would have been wise enough to ask for wisdom in the first place," suggested the Queen shrewdly.

Then he gave her presents even more valuable than those she had brought him, and she returned home saying that Solomon's wisdom was as inexhaustible as the sands of the seashore and his soul as full of poetry as the flowing sea.

Three thousand proverbs and a thousand songs poured from his lips, and were recorded by his scribes, words of wisdom, words of love and a celebration of life.

But loving beauty, Solomon also loved beautiful women – one thousand of them, from several nations. Some did not worship God, and encouraged Solomon to follow their own religions – in short to betray the god of Israel. For that reason, God little by little took back the gifts he had given to Solomon – though not in his lifetime. He took back the peace, the prosperity, even at last the lovely Temple itself, as Solomon's heirs squabbled over the kingdom like those two mothers and, in their foolishness, tore it in half.

ELIJAH THE PROPHET

AFTER SOLOMON DIED, the Kingdom of Israel was split between rival kings and, for twenty-two years, Ahab ruled over the Samarian half. If Solomon was the best of kings, then Ahab was the worst. And he married a woman whose evil surpassed even his own. Her name was Jezebel, and she worshipped the sky-god, Baal. So fond was she of her wicked religion, that she had the prophets of the true God murdered by the hundred, by the tens of hundreds, until only one was left in Israel: Elijah.

The sky saw such sights, then, as to make it weep with sorrow. But the sky did not weep. Every last cloud melted away, and God sent drought on the people as a punishment. At first, Elijah, hiding on the banks of the river Jordan, was kept alive by ravens who daily brought him bread and meat. But then the river dried up and Elijah had nothing to drink. Following God's instructions, he went to the city of Zarephath and there, by the city gates, he asked a poor woman for water and something to eat.

"Sir, I have nothing myself! A handful of flour and a last drop of oil. I was gathering firewood to cook them into one last meal for me and my son, before we sit down together and starve." But she took the prophet home, even so, and when he asked again for the last of her flour and oil, gave it him.

"Neither your jar of flour nor your bottle of oil will empty until the days of drought and famine are over, for you have been good to one of God's prophcts," Elijah told her, and the jar and the bottle lasted and lasted. If only the woman's happiness could have lasted as long. Next day she found her son dead and, picking up his little body in her arms, howled at the brazen sky in misery. "Is this my reward for sheltering a prophet of the God of Israel?"

*Cry aloud: for he is
a god; either he is
talking, or he is
pursuing, or he is
in a journey, or
peradventure he
sleepeth, and must
be awaked.*

1 KINGS 18:27

Elijah took the child from her, carried him upstairs. "Oh Lord! Would you really send such calamity on the woman who helped me?" Three times he stretched himself across the limp little body, until suddenly the boy gave a cough, a shudder and struggled back to life.

"Now I know that you are truly a man of God," said the widow. Her sobbing laughter was like water bubbling from a flagon.

After this, Elijah plucked up his courage and went to King Ahab and told him roundly of his wickedness in changing the religion of Israel. He delivered a challenge, too. "Summon the false prophets of this false god Baal, and gather all the people to holy Mount Carmel to bear witness. We shall see whose God is greatest!"

Two sacrifices were prepared on the slopes of the holy mountain – one on the altar of the sky-god Baal, the other on an altar of Elijah's making. Then the prophets of the Queen's wicked religion – all four hundred and fifty of them – danced their limping, loping ritual dances and called on their pagan god: "Send down fire to eat up our sacrifice to you!" All day they danced, while Elijah smiled behind his hand and joked at their expense. "Call louder," he said. "Perhaps your god's asleep." And the prophets of Baal fairly danced themselves to a standstill, trying to fetch down fire.

Then Elijah called on God to send fire. Like the sun falling from the sky, like a comet crashing to earth, fistfuls of fire fell on Elijah's sacrifice, and everyone who saw it burn fell on their faces and shouted, "The Lord is God!"

The four hundred and fifty prophets did not stand a chance. No god "Baal" came to their rescue, and they died at the hand of Elijah, at the river's edge.

King Ahab, his cheeks red with warmth from the burning ox, waited for Elijah to tell him what to do next. "Eat and drink," said the prophet, when he returned from killing the prophets of Baal. "The drought is over."

Ahab looked at the sky. There was not so much as a cloud. But sure enough, within a matter of hours, a cloud no bigger than a man's hand formed out at sea. It blew inland, growing, swelling, rolling into a bank of black thunderclouds. As Ahab drove his chariot the seventeen miles back to his palace at Jezreel, Elijah ran ahead of it, torrential rain lifting the dust in tussocks around his running feet. The drought and famine were over.

When Ahab told his wife Jezebel about the death of the prophets of Baal, she did not fall on her face and worship God. She sent Elijah this message: "May I die too, unless I kill you within the day for what you have done!"

Elijah was terrified. His triumph turned as sour as defeat. He fled into the desert, alone and hunted, and sprawled beneath the shade of a gorse bush, wishing he were dead already. An angel

And, behold, the Lord passed by, and a great and strong wind rent the mountains, and brake in pieces the rocks before the Lord; but the Lord was not in the wind: and after the wind an earthquake; but the Lord was not in the earthquake: And after the earthquake a fire; but the Lord was not in the fire: and after the fire a still small voice.

1 KINGS 19:11, 12

came while he slept and laid water and a cake by his head. Gently shaking his shoulder, the angel said, "Eat. Drink. Or you won't have the strength to go to Horeb, the holy mountain of God."

When Elijah woke, he ate and drank and began to walk to Horeb. It took him forty days and nights, but the cake and water sustained him. On the slopes of the mountain, he stood and awaited his instructions from God.

A howling wind lashed the mountainside and shredded its greenery and felled its trees. But God was not in the wind.

An earthquake shook the mountain, till its boulders rolled and its sides split. But God was not in the earthquake.

A fire blazed, destroying the fallen trees, and charring the mountainside black. Elijah was cloaked in thick, choking smoke. But God was not in the fire. His was the still, small voice which spoke in the silence after the wind, the earthquake and the fire.

"Anoint the man called Hazael to the King over the one half of my nation. He is a good man. Anoint the man called Jehu to be King over the rest. He too is good. And anoint young Elisha to be my prophet after you are dead. These new kings you create will wipe out the kingdom of Ahab, and only those who have been true to me in the days of false worship shall be left alive."

Elijah obeyed, and everything happened just as the still, small voice had said it would. Ahab was killed in battle. No sky-god reached out of the rainclouds to save Jezebel from the angry mob who murdered her in the streets of Jezreel.

Elijah hung his cloak around the shoulders of young Elisha, and trained him up for the perilous and fearful life of a prophet. Then his work was done. As Elisha and Elijah – as close as father and son – walked beside the River Jordan, a chariot of whirling fire, drawn by horses whose manes and hooves were all aflame, dipped low out of the sky and passed between them. Elijah rode in splendour up into the sky, and Elisha was left alone, on the banks of the Jordan, bowed down by the prophet's heavy cloak.

DANIEL IN THE LION'S DEN

GOOD KINGS, bad kings, wars and peacetimes, punishments from Heaven and divine forgiveness. Little by little, the people of Israel grew unworthy of the Holy Temple and the lovely city which surrounded it. God warned them: for twenty years, His prophet Jeremiah warned of disaster, if the people did not mend their ways. But they chose to ignore his gloomy predictions. Meanwhile, far away to the east, a great empire grew up - the empire of Babylon. It overran Egypt, it captured Assyria. At last it took Judah and the holy city of Jerusalem. King Nebuchadnezzar of Babylon, when he triumphed, took captive five thousand Israelites, and stripped the Temple of its golden ornaments. The nation built up by Abraham, Moses, David and Solomon was tumbled like the Tower of Babel.

Nebuchadnezzar worshipped pagan gods. Even so, he was no barbarian. His empire was the mightiest in the world, and he surrounded himself with wise and educated men. He was cruel yet sensitive, stupid yet hungry for knowledge. Above all, Nebuchadnezzar was superstitious.

From among the captive Israelites, the most intelligent, handsome and promising boys were chosen to serve the King. Among these were four friends: Daniel, Shadrach, Meshach and Abednego. The King found them even cleverer than his own sorcerers or fortune-tellers.

At about that time he dreamt a fearful dream, woke and dared not sleep again. So he sent for his wise men: "What did my dream mean?"

"O King live for ever! Tell us what you dreamed and we will tell you what it meant," said the wise men smugly.

But the dream had slipped away out of Nebuchadnezzar's grasp, as dreams do on waking. All he could remember was the worry left behind. "You must tell me what I dreamed as well as what it meant!"

"But nobody can do that!" protested the wise men.

"Excuses! Excuses! Fools masquerading as wise men! You'll all die for this! Every wise man in Babylon shall die!"

But Daniel the Israelite came to the rescue. "I will explain the dream!" he told the Captain of the Guard. The Captain of the Guard rushed Daniel to the palace like a bucket of water to a fire.

"O King live for ever! That same God who laid the dream on your pillow has told me what you dreamed and what the dream meant," said Daniel. "You dreamed of a vast statue – the figure of a man with a golden head, chest and arms of silver, stomach and thighs of brass, legs of iron and feet of clay. A stone struck the feet of clay and smashed them, so that the whole statue tottered, fell and broke into fragments. Your dream was a message from God. The golden head represents you, for God has sent you to rule over a mighty and marvellous empire. But after your kingdom will come another not so wonderful – an age of silver, so to speak. After that will come a third, part iron, part clay. All these great empires will fall. Only the kingdom God builds will never be destroyed."

Nebuchadnezzar took the news well. Part flattered, part amazed, he lavished gifts and honours on Daniel and granted the favour he asked: that Shadrach, Meshach and Abednego be made important officials of state. You can imagine how pleased the Babylonians were to see Israelite captives holding the highest posts in the land! Some were so jealous that they began plotting against Shadrach, Meshach and Abednego. (Daniel was too close to the King.)

Perhaps the dregs of his dream lived on in Nebuchadnezzar's mind, for a few years later he took it into his head to build a great golden statue twenty times the size of a man. He set it up on a

Did not we cast three men bound into the midst of the fire? . . . Lo, I see four men loose, walking in the midst of the fire, and they have no hurt; and the form of the fourth is like the Son of God.

DANIEL 3:24, 25

plain, and people came from all over the world to wonder at it.

But it was more than a statue. It was an idol. Nebuchadnezzar wanted people to worship it. At the sound of trumpets, everyone in Babylon was to fall down before the golden idol – *or burn.*

Of course Shadrach, Meshach and Abednego would do no such thing. They knew there was only one God – invisible, everywhere and far more precious than gold. And God's Law forbad them to worship any idol at all. So they ignored the trumpets.

Their enemies – those same jealous Chaldeans – went whining to Nebuchadnezzar. "O King live for ever! Didn't you say that anyone who refused to worship your golden idol must be thrown into a burning fiery furnace? Well, Shadrach, Meshach and Abednego refuse to bow down when the trumpets blow!"

"Fetch them here!" commanded the King.

Shadrach, Meshach and Abednego explained. "We *can't* bow down to your golden idol. We worship the one true God and He forbids it . . . And He will take care of those who obey His law."

Nebuchadnezzar's fearful temper flared up. "Stoke the furnace! Heat it seven times hotter than ever! Then throw them in!"

Then and there, the three Israelites were tied up and dragged away to the furnace – a pit of fire burning so ferociously that the strong men who bundled the prisoners to the brink were killed by the heat belching through the open door – but not before they had pitched their helpless prisoners into the flames.

The King sat as close as he dared, to watch the grisly entertainment. His eyes fixed on the red glare, he suddenly exclaimed, "Weren't there *three* men thrown in? Why can I count *four*? Their ropes are untied and they're . . . they're just . . . *walking about!* And the fourth one . . . he looks so . . . almost like a god . . ." Could it be true that the God of Shadrach, Meshach and Abednego had come in person to save them from the flames? "Shadrach! Meshach! Abednego!" called the King. "Come out of the fire!"

And out came the three friends. Not a hair of their heads, not

a hem of their clothing was so much as singed. They did not even smell of smoke. No fourth man emerged, but inside the furnace, bright, leaping flames flapped like the wings of an angel.

Then Nebuchadnezzar saw how the God of the Israelites compared with his idols and images, and he made a proclamation: "Let no man say a bad word about this God of theirs. No other God has such powers!" And he made the three still more important and powerful – to the fury of their enemies.

The age of gold ended. Nebuchadnezzar died, and his son Belshazzar was a lesser man than his father. He prayed to idols made of gold and silver, bronze, iron and wood. He even used the holy chalices captured from the temple in Jerusalem as drinking goblets - they stood on the table when, one day, Belshazzar threw a riotous feast.

In the middle of the party, the laughing suddenly stopped, the singing fell silent, the clatter and chatter died away. A hand – a hand without an arm – appeared in mid-air and began to write

*And this is the
writing that was
written, MENE,
MENE, TEKEL,
UPHARSIN.*

DANIEL 5:25

*This is the
interpretation of the
thing: MENE;
God hath numbered
thy kingdom, and
finished it.
TEKEL; Thou art
weighed in the
balances, and art
found wanting.*

DANIEL 5:26, 27

on the wall these strange words: *MENE, MENE, TEKEL,
UPHARSIN.*

The King's face went white. His legs shook. "What does it
mean?" But no one could say.

"Send for that Israelite, Daniel!" suggested the Queen, and
when he came Belshazzar offered him all manner of rewards if he
could explain the writing on the wall.

Bravely, Daniel did just that. "You can keep your presents,
Belshazzar. Your father Nebuchadnezzar learned to honour the
one true God. But you have gone back to worshipping idols.
You've used the holy vessels out of His Temple for drinking your
wine, and you've ignored the God who made you what you are
today. This is what the writing means: Your kingdom is at an
end. You have been weighed in the scales and found too light.
God is giving your kingdom to the Medes and Persians."

That same night, Belshazzar was killed. Babylon was attacked
by foreign invaders – the Medes and Persians – and Darius the
Mede became King.

King Darius found that he, too, liked, admired and trusted
Daniel, and he made him one of just three Presidents to rule over
the country. Now Medes, Persians and Babylonians alike all hated
and resented this upstart Israelite, and they plotted his downfall.

Wickedly, they suggested to Darius that no one should "pray"
to anyone but the King . . . on pain of being thrown to the lions!
Flattered, Darius signed their unholy decree. But of course Daniel
would pray to no one but God. His enemies went tattling to the
King: "Didn't you decree that no one must pray to anyone but
you?"

"I did."

"And that anyone who disobeyed should be thrown to the
lions?"

"I did, but who . . . ?"

"And are not the laws of the Medes and Persians unalterable?"

"Yes, yes, but who has disobeyed my decree?"

When Darius heard that it was Daniel, he was very sorry indeed. He racked his brains for some way of saving his friend, but it was no use. Daniel was dragged to the mouth of a pit full of ravenous, roaring lions. "May your God come to your rescue!" cried the unhappy king as Daniel was tumbled into the pit. Then a stone was rolled across the mouth of the den.

Darius could not sleep that night for picturing Daniel, mauled and eaten by the lions. He got up early and went to the den. "Daniel! Daniel! Was your God able to save you?"

Daniel's calm voice replied: "O King live for ever! God sent an angel to shut the lions' mouths."

DANIEL IN THE LION'S DEN

And the king spake and said to Daniel, O Daniel, servant of the living God, is thy God, whom thou servest continually, able to deliver thee from the lions?
Then said Daniel unto the king, O king, live for ever. My God hath sent his angel, and hath shut the lions' mouths . . .
DANIEL 6:20, 21, 22

He delivereth and rescueth, and he worketh signs and wonders in heaven and in earth, who hath delivered Daniel from the power of the lions.
DANIEL 6:27

Delightedly, Darius ordered the pit to be opened, and in place of Daniel, Daniel's accusers were thrown inside. (This time the hungry lions were not so slow to begin their meal.) Then Darius wrote letters to all corners of his empire commanding his subjects to worship the only God whose hand could muzzle a pride of lions.

It was Daniel's turn to dream dreams − visions of beasts and winds and kingdoms and of times far in the future. Some he understood, and some even he could not fathom. Wearily he asked God, "How will it all end?"

God told him, "Write down your visions, Daniel, and then it is time for you to rest. The wise will understand you and the wicked will pay no heed. Only Time can turn the future into the present."

There was to be another cave, sealed with a stone and full of Death, from which God released a man alive . . . But even Daniel was not permitted to see quite so far into the future.

ESTHER SPEAKS FOR HER PEOPLE

"CALL QUEEN VASHTI! Have her come before the King!" But Queen Vashti did not come. She sent word that she was busy. Such was the might of the King of Persia, such was the awe he struck in the hearts of men, that no one ever disobeyed. So when Queen Vashti, his wife, was summoned, and Queen Vashti did not come, King Ahasuerus banished her and looked elsewhere for a queen. He sent word for all the most beautiful girls to be brought to the palace, so that he could choose the one who pleased him best.

Esther was among those young women taken to the palace. She was a Jewish orphan – one of the countless thousand Israelites who had made their home within the vast bounds of the Persian Empire. Raised by the kindness of old Mordecai, she loved him as much as any father. "Tell no one that you are an Israelite – a Jew," Mordecai warned her, and she followed his advice and kept silent about her background – even when King Ahasuerus chose her for his new queen from among all the girls in the land!

Now the King had a grand vizier called Haman, who thought himself as fine as the King himself. He gave himself such airs that he decreed everyone should bow down as he walked by. Swaggering one day through the King's Gate, Haman noticed how the old Jew, Mordecai, did not bow down. In his vanity, Haman swore vengeance. But rather than punish the one man, he condemned the whole Jewish race.

He presented a plea to King Ahasuerus. "On the thirteenth day of the twelfth month, let the Jews be destroyed – man, woman and child, in every province of your great Empire! For they are a wicked race who have their own laws and refuse to keep yours."

The King, believing him, said, "Do as you see fit."

When Mordecai learned the fate in store for the Jews, he tore his clothes and wept. He could see only one solution; Esther must beg the King to show mercy and forbid the massacre. But marriage to King Ahasuerus was not like any other marriage. So great was this Emperor, so envied, so legendary, so godlike a figure, that he lived solitary, like an idol in a temple. If he summoned a person, they might come into his presence; if he did not, no one approached, on pain of death, for they might be an enemy, an assassin, a usurper. Ahasuerus trusted no one. Not even his wife.

"I daren't go to him," said Esther, when Mordecai asked her help. "Not unless he sends for me!"

"You must! You are our only hope!"

Esther was silent. She pictured the vast and varied Empire over which her husband reigned – from the valley of the Indus to the deserts of Nubia, pictured the metal-clad soldiers going from

house to house, routing out Jews – man, woman and child –
spilling their blood. "I will do it," she said, "even if it costs me
my life."

So Esther combed and perfumed her hair, then walked the
long passageway to the great pavement which lay like a sea around
the mighty throne. The eyes of Ahasuerus rested on her as she
slowly approached across the marble floor. Suddenly he stretched
out his golden sceptre. He had granted her permission to speak.

"What favour have you to ask of me, Queen Esther, for I
have a mind to grant it!" said the King, affably.

Esther laid her hand on the golden sceptre. "Then let the
King and his grand vizier Haman come to dinner tonight, and let
me ask my favour then."

The King readily agreed. So did Haman, who was already
greatly pleased with how the day was going. Outside in the
courtyard, in accordance with his orders, stood a gallows fifteen

*Then Esther the
queen answered
and said, If I have
found favour in thy
sight, O king, and
if it please the king,
let my life be given
me at my petition,
and my people at
my request . . .*
ESTHER 7:3

metres high. It was the gibbet on which the odious Mordecai was to hang next day. Never again would Haman have to look at the old Jew sitting, day after day, by the King's Gate, glaring at him with his dark accusing eyes. Yes, Haman's day was going well. Now dinner, too!

Esther's dinner was a delight of tastes and smells. Ahasuerus grew mellow as the evening wore on, and asked what favour Esther could possibly ask of him that he would refuse. His young wife stood up, as lovely and as timid as a gazelle, trembling, wide-eyed.

"The favour I ask is my life, and the lives of all my people."

The King was astounded. "Why? Who wants to kill you?"

Esther pointed a trembling finger. "That man there. That wicked Haman. For I am a Jew and he means to slaughter every Jewish man, woman and child to satisfy his pride and spite. He lied, and slandered a race of good people out of sheer malice."

Then Ahasuerus looked between wife and vizier, between beauty and wickedness, between a bold young woman and a scheming old man, and he judged between them.

That is how Haman came to be hanged on the tall, tall gallows in the courtyard, and how Mordecai lived to carry the news to his people – that the Jews of the Persian Empire were free to live and laugh again, everywhere from the Indus Valley to the deserts of Nubia.

JONAH AND THE GREAT FISH

HE WAS NO ELIJAH. He was no Elisha. He was no daring prophet ready to lay down his life doing the Lord's business. In fact, when Jonah heard God's voice telling him to preach to the city of Nineveh, he would rather have done anything, gone anywhere than go to Nineveh. Tell a city full of people that they were annoying the Lord God? Tell thousands that they risked death and destruction if they did not change their ways?

Not if he could help it.

Jonah took ship for Tarshish, the longest sea voyage available, hoping that God would not see which way he had gone. But as King David wrote in one of his songs,

Though I run to the ends of the earth,
or hide in the uttermost parts of the sea,
even there God will find me, His hand hold me.

There was to be no escape.

A storm blew up which pitched the ship as high as the rainclouds, then plunged it deep into black folds of sea.

"What's happening? What have we done to deserve this?" howled the sailors, sensing, with superstitious dread, that the storm was a punishment. The planks groaned, the seams split, leaks spurted in a hundred different places. The sailors threw the cargo overboard, but still the ship sank lower and lower in the racing roar of water.

"It's me," said Jonah. "Throw me into the sea, and the wind will drop. I am a servant of the Lord God, and I've disobeyed my master."

Arise, go to Nineveh, that great city, and cry against it . . .
JONAH 1:2

*So they took up
Jonah, and cast
him forth into the
sea: and the sea
ceased from her
raging.*
JONAH 1:15

*Then Jonah prayed
unto the Lord his
God out of the
fish's belly,
And said, I cried
by reason of mine
affliction unto the
Lord, and he heard
me; out of the belly
of hell cried I, and
thou heardest my
voice.*
JONAH 2:1, 2

The sailors were loath to throw anyone overboard, but they had exhausted every other possibility. The sails hung in tatters, the bilges were full. So they took hold regretfully – apologetically – of Jonah, and dropped him over the side. At once the storm ceased.

Down and down Jonah sank, as though his soul was lead-weighted. His lungs burned, his mouth loosed a scream of silver bubbles. The light of day faded out of sight above him. Then, just when he thought it was as dark as darkness can be, a greater dark overwhelmed him, closed round him, enveloped him in a fleshy cave. He had been swallowed by a monstrous fish!

It could not have been a whale, surely, for a whale's throat is too small to swallow a man. And yet its ribs were like the vaulted arches of a great building, its backbone like the crossbeam of a barn. Jonah stood ankle-deep in rotting fish and krill, and the stench felled him to his knees.

Even so, it dawned on Jonah – as much as anything can dawn on a man wrapped in pitchy darkness – that God had saved him from drowning. "O God, my deliverer! Where can a man go that you won't reach out a hand to save him? Will you free me from this vile prison to be your prophet on blessed dry land, or is this my death sentence for disobeying you?"

As if in answer, the gigantic fish gave a shudder, and ran aground. Its mouth gaped, and daylight flooded in, as it vomited up Jonah amid a foul cascade of decomposing fish.

"*Now* will you go to Nineveh?" asked God.

Filled with a new zeal, Jonah went at once – to the great city of Nineveh – a thriving metropolis of shops, houses, palaces and temples. He stood up in the King's court and he threatened storms of fire, torrents of brimstone, death, destruction and misery.

And they listened to him!

"He's right! We must change our ways," said the King, "or God will very probably do as this good man says! Fast, everyone!

Pray and do penance, and let's beg forgiveness for disappointing the Lord God! Perhaps even at this late hour, He will forgive us!"

Jonah meanwhile sat down, at some safe distance from the city, and waited for destruction to rain down on it.

"I've decided to forgive them," said the Lord.

Jonah was *furious*. Well, it made him look such a fool – to promise destruction and have none fall from the sky. He sat in a huddle and sulked.

"Did you really think," said God, amused, "that I would destroy a city of this size – all those men and women and children, not to mention the animals, when it was trying so hard to do better? Did you?"

"Pah!" said Jonah, scowling, and stomped home, leaving behind him the sound of Nineveh's grateful psalms rising like larks on the morning air.

RETURNING HOME

MANY PROPHETS had predicted the fall of Babylon: some had been believed, some not. For how could such an empire crumble or surrender? When at last a new warlord fixed his ambitions on the city of hanging gardens, Babylon fell quickly and utterly.

The latest conqueror decreed that the captive Jews should be allowed to go home, to practise their own religion, even to rebuild their beloved temple which lay in ruins. How the Jews rejoiced at the news! To be going home! But it was twenty years before the renovated Temple stood at the centre of Holy Jerusalem again: the heart of Jewish life was beating once more.

The prophets spoke, too, of God sending a man. Someone was coming down the corridors of Time, to raise up and glorify the nation of the Jews. Soon, soon, they would see him: a Messiah, a Saviour, a ruler far greater than any king. The prophets spoke of him and were believed. But who this Messiah would be, and what he would achieve taxed the wisdom of many scholars and stirred debate among the old men who sat in the Temple and talked of God's intentions.

And how long would they have to wait? One year? Ten years? A hundred years? It was as though, in each house, a table had been laid to welcome a guest – a guest who did not arrive.

The voice of him that crieth in the wilderness, Prepare ye the way of the Lord, make straight in the desert a highway for our God.
Every valley shall be exalted, and every mountain and hill shall be made low: and the crooked shall be made straight, and the rough places plain:
And the glory of the Lord shall be revealed . . .
ISAIAH 40:3, 4, 5

For five hundred years they waited, and by then, no one was any longer sure what they wanted, or what to expect. "A shepherd," said one prophet, "born in Bethlehem." But when a man finally came, some said, "Yes! this is he!" while others said, "No, we will wait a while longer: there will be another along soon." Waiting had become a way of life.

The story of the man who came – Jesus of Nazareth – fills another whole book which is called The New Testament.